A CRASH COURSE ON CRISES

A Crash Course on Crises

MACROECONOMIC CONCEPTS FOR RUN-UPS, COLLAPSES, AND RECOVERIES

MARKUS K. BRUNNERMEIER
RICARDO REIS

PRINCETON UNIVERSITY PRESS

PRINCETON & OXFORD

Published by Princeton University Press
41 William Street, Princeton, New Jersey 08540
99 Banbury Road, Oxford OX2 6JX

press.princeton.edu

All Rights Reserved
ISBN 978-0-691-22110-6
ISBN (e-book) 978-0-691-22111-3

British Library Cataloging-in-Publication Data is available

Editorial: Joe Jackson, Josh Drake and Whitney Rauenhorst
Production Editorial: Jenny Wolkowicki
Jacket design: Drohan DiSanto
Production: Erin Suydam
Publicity: William Pagdatoon
Copyeditor: Bhisham Bherwani

This book has been composed in Arno Pro

10 9 8 7 6 5 4 3 2 1

CONTENTS

1

Introduction

THE UNITED STATES' financial crisis of 2008–10 and the euro area's sovereign debt crisis of 2010–12 were stark examples of how financial crashes can bring down whole economies. Unlike in previous decades, these crashes were not limited to wild gyrations in asset prices nor to great gains and losses for sharks and fools. They did not only afflict countries where institutional problems and clear fault lines in the way financial markets operate make a crisis a matter of time. Rather, these were *macro-financial* crises. They brought economic hardship to households throughout the world, in rich and emerging countries alike. Financial economists have naturally exerted much effort understanding manias and panics in financial markets, while macroeconomists have always been just as busy making sense of great recessions and depressions.

Over the last decade, instead, there has been an enormous amount of research at the intersection of macroeconomics and finance devoted to times when financial markets and the macroeconomy move violently. Researchers have explored new ideas, new evidence, and new explanations for what we saw, and applied them to not just recent global crises, but also to make sense of regional crashes over the previous 30 years. This book provides a short introduction to some of these ideas.

1.1   Crashes

There are a bewildering number of financial markets. In each of them, people trade in different assets, in different regions, with different counterparties. Asset prices are naturally volatile as they respond to myriad changes in fundamentals, institutional features, and people's beliefs. It is therefore no surprise that, at any point in time, some financial market somewhere will be going through a sharp slump in prices or in volumes of trading.

A financial crisis is much more than this. It is a time when many financial markets show the same pattern of losses, when bad news in one corner quickly spreads to several others, and when one institution's failures make it default on commitments to others, all struck like a row of dominoes. A macro-financial crash is even more than this. It happens when the financial troubles spill to the real economy and back into financial troubles. These crises come with sharp and deep recessions, where millions lose their jobs, income falls, and democratic institutions come under pressure to find others to blame. These crashes are the topic of this book.

While they are extreme in their consequences, crashes are not rare. In the last two decades alone, the two major macroeconomic events affecting many countries at once—the global recession of 2008–10 and the euro area troubles in 2010–12—were macro-financial crashes. So were some of the largest falls in well-being in isolated countries, from Argentina to Turkey to Lebanon. The pandemic recession of 2020–21 threatened to evolve into a new macro-financial crisis, but the financial markets bounced back and the economy showed resilience, even if leading ultimately to high inflation. Similarly, the Russian invasion into Ukraine in February 2022 and subsequent sanctions could have triggered a financial crisis and may still do so. Naturally, economists have worked to figure out why these crashes happen in the first place, how they spread, and how we can mitigate their effects. With this knowledge, scientists can understand why crashes are a feature of modern economies, and policymakers can be prepared to try to prevent them and respond to them when they happen. Like viruses, financial crises and recessions cannot be eradicated. But, just as scientists strive to learn how viral outbreaks can become pandemics and how to contain them, so do economists when it comes to macro-financial crises.

Unsurprisingly, new concepts to understand these crashes have been developed. Notwithstanding, they are only vaguely known to economists working outside the intersection of macroeconomics and financial economics. Students of economics at the undergraduate and, often, masters levels are for the most part unaware of them. The modern study of crashes has not yet seeped through to textbooks. As a result, in public debates or policy discussions, crashes are sometimes still referred to as aberrations in economic science. Even when people use modern concepts and models of crashes, they often lack an understanding of how they precisely work, how they can be applied, and how they fit together. The goal of this book is to introduce these ideas at the intersection of macroeconomics and finance. Together they provide a richer account of past crashes and offer insights into potential future crashes.

The book has ten main chapters, each being mostly self-contained and dedicated to one idea. In turn, each chapter is split into three integrated sections. The first introduces one concept in macro-finance aided by one diagram. The second and third apply this concept to two different historical crashes. We rely on intuition, diagrams, and plots, as opposed to formal models, derivations, or econometrics. Our approach is analytical, but we presume only a solid class in introduction to economics from the reader. Every section presents one insight, from a model or a historical event, rather than a discussion of alternatives or an account of the many other factors that would paint a full picture. We attempt to be brief and sharp, while being aware that each of the 30 sections can be expanded into a whole book in itself. Our goal is not to provide a survey for researchers, but rather to provide an entry point to the literature that teachers and students can use in classes to supplement their textbooks. In short, we have tried to provide a crash course on crashes.

1.2   Organization of the Book

The book is split into three parts: i) the run-up to a macro-financial crisis, ii) its trigger, spread, and amplification, and lastly, iii) the recovery and the policies around it.

The first part focuses on the features that feed a crisis. Chapter 2 discusses people's beliefs in a world of pervasive uncertainty about fundamentals as well as about what others will do. These beliefs can sometimes lead to large capital flows toward risky assets, and to swift rises in asset prices. Even if anyone looking at the financial market concludes that there is a bubble, elevated asset prices can persist. But at some point, they no longer do, and what follows is often a violent crash. We explain this by introducing concepts of backward induction, higher-order beliefs, and beauty contests.

The first application is to the Japanese land and stock market bubble of the late 1990s. Its crash was followed by 30 years during which the Japanese economy grew at a significantly slower pace than it had grown during 1955–85. The second application is to the Internet (or dot-com) asset price bubble of 1998–2000, when technological changes came with real investments but also great uncertainty in assessing the fundamental value of financial assets. During this time, sophisticated investors did not lean against the rapidly rising asset prices but rather rode the bubble. Given the uncertainty, each one individually found this profitable, even if it risked triggering a financial crisis.

Most crashes are also preceded by a rush of capital into the country. The capital flows are drawn by a desire to ride the bubble, and often come in response to financial liberalization or optimism about future growth. Commentators divide themselves between those that applaud the reallocation of capital from rich places to regions that have more potential for growth, and those that warn of dangers and condemn foolish excesses. Chapter 3 introduces the concept of capital misallocation. It explains how large capital flows can be allocated away from sectors where rewards would be higher, and from the most productive firms. Some economic growth can disguise stagnant productivity and zombie firms.

The first application is to the Portuguese slump in the twenty-first century. The euro, and the integration of financial markets in the euro area that came with it, led to large capital flows into the country, which promised prosperity. Instead, the Portuguese economy slumped between 2001 and 2008, and then crashed. Portugal has had its lowest 20-year period of economic growth in the last 140 years. Similar stories apply to Greece and Spain during this period. The second application is to Chile's economy in the 1970s, when a fast-paced financial liberalization and economic growth came to a sudden crash in 1982. Argentina and Uruguay went through a similar, but less dramatic, experience. These crashes in the Southern Cone triggered the first wave of the economic literature on misallocation. The particular experience of Chile is notable because it comes intertwined with the Pinochet regime, which many readers will know about from history books.

The third chapter of this first section introduces the reader to modern financial institutions. Whether they are called banks, shadow banks, or something else, they share the feature of creating liquidity but being prone to runs. The chapter focuses on their balance sheets and how they get funded. This includes a discussion of the incentives for bankers to monitor and manage loans prudently. It also explains how financial institutions obtain their resources from both funders directly as well as from markets, and how the two sources expose them to different risks.

The first application is the housing boom and crash in the United States in 2000–07. We discuss how in the run-up to the crisis, U.S. banks securitized their mortgages to an unprecedented extent, and how this allowed for a credit boom. The second application is on the other side of the Atlantic. During this time, the Spanish banking sector experienced the rise of a sub-sector, the "Cajas," which over the prior decades had been relatively stagnant. They mostly dedicated themselves to real estate lending, and their growth came with the rise of a new financial product, mortgage-backed securities, which they supplied in great amounts. Their story has many common elements with the savings and loans crisis of the 1980s United States, or with the rise and fall of Northern Rock in the United Kingdom in the 2000s.

The second part of the book studies the arrival of a crisis. Each chapter introduces a different trigger or amplifier of a crash. Chapter 5 starts with how small shocks can get amplified and become systemic through the links that connect different financial institutions. These links lead to strategic complementarities, a concept that pervades most accounts of runs and crashes. In some cases, they may even lead to multiple equilibria, so that even pure changes in beliefs about what others will do can trigger a crash. The link to the real economy enhances these connections because a fall in lending creates the losses that trigger new rounds of lending cuts.

The first application deals with the 2007–08 banking crisis in Ireland. It discusses how Irish banks became systemic between the 1990s and the 2000s, tied by their common investments in real estate and common sources of funding. The second application deals with the global crisis in 1997–98. Financial troubles that first led to crises in Indonesia, Malaysia, Thailand, and the Philippines triggered crises in Hong Kong, Korea, and Singapore just a few months later. A few more months went by, and the crisis spread to Russia, followed by Brazil, and then Argentina, Chile, Colombia, Mexico, and Venezuela. The crisis was globally systemic, connecting countries that were alike and unalike in similar ways.

Most capital flows across borders through debt contracts. One important property of debt contracts is that they give rise to a definition of the economic solvency of the borrower. Solvency depends on the perception about the future surpluses of an institution, which is studied in chapter 6. The value today of these surpluses depends on the interest rate used to discount them. When interest rates spike, a solvent institution can become illiquid, unable to roll over and service its debt, even though its surpluses have not changed. An outside institution with deep pockets, like the IMF, can eliminate the illiquidity outcomes, but it has to distinguish them from insolvency, a difficult task.

Our first application is to the Greek sovereign crisis of 2010–12, and explores how a series of events that blurred the distinction between insolvency and illiquidity led to Greece's gradual inability to roll over its debt and, in spite of the IMF's role, culminated in a sovereign default. The second application is to the failure of an Austrian bank in 1931 and how it contributed to the arrival of the Great Depression in Europe.

While chapters 5 and 6 focus on the servicing of debt by financial institutions and sovereigns, respectively, chapter 7 turns to the link between the two. Bank funding and public debt are tightly linked. From one direction, banking crises typically come with large fiscal costs. Governments find themselves directly bailing out the banks while collecting fewer taxes and spending more on social payments during the recession. From the other direction, when public debt is riskier, its value falls, and the banks that hold this debt see their balance sheets suffer. This creates a diabolic, or doom, loop tying financial institutions and governments.

Our first application is to European banks in Cyprus, Greece, Ireland, and Italy since 2010. In the previous decade, many of these banks grew large in size, especially relative to the size of the state they are based in, as they took advantage of the E.U. common market and the common currency. Yet, when trouble hit, it was individual states that found themselves on the hook. The second application is the Argentinian crisis of 2001. When governments have trouble rolling over their public debt, a common response is to use their power over domestic banks to have them buy this debt. This form of financial repression was common for decades well before the Argentina crisis, but the events of 2001 illustrate it well.

The final chapter in this section defines the concept of safe assets and discusses another important phenomenon in macro-financial crises: the flight to safety. In a crash, even as the perceived risk across regions, sectors, and institutions rises, the interest rate in some other regions or assets becomes unusually low. Investors shift their portfolios away from the risky assets, and toward assets that they deem safe, even if the relative safety differences are very small. As they fly to safety, they increase the liquidity of the safe asset, and make its price rise, which justifies its perceived safety in the first place. The safety of an asset is in part self-fulfilling.

Our first application is to the euro area sovereign debt crisis of 2010–12, and the flight to safety from the European periphery to its core. While prior to the euro crisis all sovereign bonds were deemed safe, with the onset of this event peripheral countries' government bonds lost their safe asset status. We moved from a risk-on to a risk-off regime. The second application is to the flight of capital from emerging markets to the United States in the second quarter of 2020. These flows occurred despite the fact that, relative to most emerging economies, the United States at the time was more heavily affected by the pandemic, its economy was suffering more under lockdown measures, and its government finances were under more strain.

The third and final part of the book discusses economic policy responses and how they affect the shape of recoveries. Chapter 9 starts with exchange-rate policies. In a macro-financial crisis, a depreciation of the exchange rate boosts exports, but it also hurts the balance sheets of domestic borrowers if they had borrowed in foreign currency beforehand. The chapter discusses this currency mismatch, the channels for these balance sheet effects, and the financial amplification of the effects. The effects may be larger than the conventional boost that a depreciated exchange rate gives to the trade balance of the country. In that case, some capital controls and foreign exchange interventions may be merited.

We apply these ideas first to the Mexican crisis of 1994. It illustrates the extent of dollarization in many emerging economies, and how it interacts with the depreciation of the exchange rate in a crash to amplify the downturn. The second application is to the worldwide recovery from the 2008–10 global recession. This was the largest global macro-financial crash since the Great Depression. It left scars that impeded a full recovery for a long time. We discuss these scars and show how slow the recovery has been to the point of suggesting that the trend growth of the economy became permanently lower.

Chapter 10 turns to monetary policy. In the decade since the global financial crisis, central banks of almost all advanced economies have adopted two new policies. First, they have increased the size of their balance sheets to satiate the higher, and more volatile, demand for central bank reserves. Secondly, they have used forward guidance and quantitative easing to lower long-term interest rates and stimulate the investment that the crises might have depressed. These policies have been named "unconventional." However, they have been around for so long, and have been so much more active than the old conventional policy of raising and lowering of short-term interest rates, that understanding them is essential to making sense of what central banks are all about today.

Our first application turns to the Bank of Japan, which since 1998 has been at the forefront of all these changes in monetary policy. Our second application is the ECB between 2008 and 2015. Unlike the Federal Reserve or Bank of England, which adopted these policies as packages, the ECB did them one at a time, making it easier to describe them and see their impacts.

Finally, chapter 11 turns to fiscal policy. A main role of financial markets is to match savers with investment opportunities. The price at which this happens is referred to as r^*, the interest rate where savings meet investment in a long-run equilibrium. Macro-financial crises, both their causes and their effects, affect what this r^* is. This chapter introduces the concepts of dynamic inefficiency and precautionary savings in discussing the forces affecting r^*, and how these change during financial crises. Fiscal policy, by determining public savings, can be used to affect r^*, especially in the functioning of its automatic stabilizers. Their effectiveness depends on the extent to which government spending crowds out private investment.

The first application is to the savings rate in the United States, the European Union, and the United Kingdom at the end of 2020, and explores what this implies for the likelihood that the pandemic evolves into a macro-financial crisis. The second application is to the recovery of the United States from the Great Depression in the 1930s, and explores the role that fiscal deficits played in it, both through the New Deal, and through military spending associated with World War II.

1.3 Uses of the Book

We had in mind two audiences when writing this book. The first is undergraduate or masters students in economics. Over the years, we have used this book to supplement existing textbooks when teaching classes in intermediate macroeconomics and in money and banking. Every chapter is self-contained, so that instructors can choose which concepts and chapters to use in their classes. We relegate links between the different chapters to endnotes, so readers wanting those connections spelled out can find them there. We assume familiarity only with introductory economics and we pedagogically illustrate economic concepts rather than present them in their generality.

Alternatively, the book could be used as a whole to teach a term-length class in macro-finance. Professional economists wanting to catch up on how research development in these fields fits together should find the book useful as well. We provide slides in our websites to accompany the book, as well as the data sources and calculations behind each figure, so they can be reproduced, modified, and extended.

The second audience is policymakers and members of the informed public wanting to absorb some of the concepts that should be guiding both macroeconomic and financial policy. The book is written as an entryway to their literatures. The discussion is qualitative, isolating economic forces, but stopping short of quantifying them. We discuss many historical episodes with the goal of sharply illustrating the concepts.

One alternative approach to the material is to skip the crisis applications and get a more theoretical primer on the ingredients of macro-financial crises. Another alternative for those who want to study one particular historical crisis more thoroughly is to look at that section of this book alone to see one economic force in isolation. Whichever way the book is used, we believe that building a good understanding of what was behind a crisis should guide the efforts to prevent another one from arising.

We tried hard to keep the book mercifully short. While we cover much ground, the writing is terse, the analytic discussions are not exhaustive, and we keep all historical details behind each crisis to the bare minimum. If the more curious readers reach the end not fully satisfied and wanting to read more, we will claim success. We use endnotes in each chapter to point to a few readings that elaborate on the models or on the historical episode. The book is not a survey, so those references do not give credit to the intellectual origins of the ideas. They are suggestions on what to read next.[1]

1.4   Acknowledgments

In 2010, we participated in a discussion group on the sovereign debt crisis in Europe, together with Luis Garicano, Philip Lane, Sam Langfield, Marco Pagano, Tano Santos, David Thesmar, Stijn Van Nieuwerburgh, and Dimitri Vayanos. They greatly shaped our initial views on macro-financial crises. We then taught generations of students at Columbia University, the London School of Economics, and Princeton University from initial drafts of this material over many years. They gave us brutally honest comments, convinced us that short is better than comprehensive, and especially motivated us to keep on working on this project. Joseph Abadi, Brendan Kehoe, Ciaran Marshall, Joe Marshall, Sebastian Merkel, Nika Vahcic, Annie Wang, and Ziqiao Zhang read through drafts of the book and provided many helpful suggestions for improvement. In the final stage, Adrien Couturier, Kaman Lyu, and Rui Sousa provided excellent research assistance, collecting data, surveying literatures, and tirelessly editing our writing. This required financial support, which we got from the European Union's Horizon 2020 research and innovation programme, INFL, under grant number No. GA: 682288.

Note

1. The closest books to ours are, perhaps, Kindleberger (1978), Montiel (2014), and Reinhart and Rogoff (2009), as they also introduce theories around macro-financial crashes and illustrate them with historical episodes. The first two are more focussed on the case studies though, rather than the theories, and the third one is focussed on sovereign debt crises.

PART I

Growing Fragilities:
The Run-up to Crises

2

Bubbles and Beliefs

FINANCIAL CRISES and their associated crashes are often preceded by large, sometimes exponential, increases in the price of some assets, and a frenzy of speculators trying to buy and sell the assets for a quick profit. These speculative asset bubbles go far back in history. During the tulip-mania in Amsterdam in 1634–37, a tulip bulb cost more than a mansion. The South Sea bubble in the United Kingdom and the Mississippi bubble in France led to excessive speculation in 1719–20. The U.K.'s Hoare's Bank was profitably riding the South Sea bubble, and so were other investors, including Isaac Newton, though with less success. Frustrated with his trading experience, Newton concluded: "I can calculate the motions of the heavenly bodies, but not the madness of people."[1]

Sometimes, these bubbles have severe real macroeconomic implications. One famous example in the past century is the United States' "roaring '20s" that preceded the 1929 crash and the Great Depression. Also notable is the 1980s in Japan, when stock as well as house prices surged to astronomical heights before crashing, followed by three lost decades in productivity and economic growth. More recently, Internet stocks skyrocketed in the United States prior to March 2000, before plummeting, in what at the time was called "irrational exuberance." In many cases, the price decline came with not just collapses of the financial system but also sharp increases in unemployment that only slowly receded. So-called macroprudential regulation is a set of policies meant to lean against the build-up of bubbles. This chapter discusses this run-up phase, in which bubbles, imbalances, and risks build up in the background before the risk materializes and a crisis erupts.[2]

2.1   A Model of Bubbles with a Keynesian Beauty Contest

Bubbles emerge when the price of an asset exceeds fundamentals because investors believe that they can sell the asset at an even higher price to some other investor in the future. The fundamental value of an asset is given by the discounted present (marginal utility) value of its payoff streams, which are dividends for stocks, interest payments for bonds, and rents for real estate. John Maynard Keynes, in his General Theory, distinguishes investors, who buy an asset for its dividend stream (fundamental value), from speculators, who buy an asset for its resale value before the bubble pops or deflates. Hyman Minsky provided an early, informal characterization of bubbles and distinguished between different phases. An initial displacement—for example, a new technology or financial innovation—leads to expectations of increased profits and economic growth. This leads to a boom phase that is usually characterized by low volatility, credit expansion, and increases in investment. Asset prices rise, first at a slower pace but then with growing momentum. During the boom phase, the price increases start exceeding the actual fundamental improvements from the innovation. This is followed by a phase of euphoria during which investors trade the overvalued asset in a frenzy. When the price increases in an explosive fashion investors may be aware, or at least suspicious, that there may be a bubble, but they are confident that they can sell the asset to a greater fool in the future. Usually, this phase will be associated with high trading volume and price volatility. At some point, sophisticated investors start reducing their positions and realizing their profits. During this phase of profit taking there may, for a while, be enough demand from less sophisticated investors who may be new to that particular market. However, at some point prices start to fall rapidly, leading to a panic phase, when investors dump the asset.[3]

Consider a specific example with two groups of investors: irrational momentum investors, and more sophisticated investors. Momentum investors have extrapolative expectations: as the price increases, they become increasingly more optimistic and believe that the price of the asset will continue to rise. In the initial displacement phase, fundamentally good news trickles out, pushing up the price and the fundamental value of the asset. The bubble starts when increases in the fundamental value slow down but asset prices continue to rise because irrational investors with extrapolative expectations take the initial price increase as a signal that the price will rise even further. As they become increasingly bullish, they buy more, further raising the price, and confirming their (mistaken) belief that current price growth can be extrapolated into future price growth. Extrapolative expectations can also arise from new groups of investors that hear about the price increases, and want to be part of the ride.

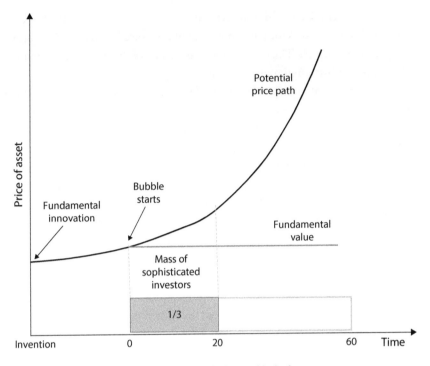

FIGURE 2.1. Bubbles and beliefs

Why don't other, more sophisticated investors, lean against the bubble, preventing it from arising in the first place? A fast growing bubble can persist because even rational investors find it more profitable to ride the bubble, especially since it requires many of them to sell at the same time to pop the bubble. This is risky since the bubble asset price might burst on them, as Isaac Newton experienced in 1720. These investors try to forecast how long the bubble will persist, which is governed by the trading behavior of the other (sophisticated) investors. A coordination problem arises, which may allow a bubble to persist. Keynes famously argued that this investment choice is reminiscent of a beauty contest, where traders are trying to pick not the most beautiful face, but the face that they think the majority of other traders find most beautiful.[4]

Figure 2.1 illustrates the bubble price path for a simple model. Assume, for concreteness, that the momentum investors with extrapolative expectations keep buying even after the price exceeds the fundamental value. They continue pushing up the price, unless a third or more of the sophisticated traders lean against them. Each of the sophisticated traders wants to ride the bubble but stop doing so just before this threshold of one third is reached, since only then will the price fall. The challenge that each one of them faces is to predict what other sophisticated traders will do.

Start with one of the sophisticated traders' initial (or first-order) belief that the other sophisticates may ride the bubble after it started for 0 periods, 60 periods, or any number in between, with an equal number of agents at each date. In this case, she would expect the bubble to burst in $(1/3) \times 60 = 20$ periods after the bubble had started. Hence, she would not want to hold the asset for more than 20 periods after the price started to exceed the fundamental. In turn, selling before then would be less profitable than riding the bubble since the extrapolative traders push up the price. As a result, she "attacks" the bubble at exactly 20 periods after the start of the bubble.

However, our individual sophisticated trader realizes that all of the other sophisticated traders make the same calculation. If so, they would all sell at the same time, after 20 periods since the inception of the bubble. Now, the first third who do so manage to get out and sell at the high prices, but the other 2/3 do it at a loss after the bubble pops. Therefore, through this second level of reasoning, she concludes she should sell instead in period 19, realizing a (slightly smaller) sure gain instead of going for the slightly higher gain with only a one out of three chance. Again, though, she realizes others might reason the same way. Through third level reasoning, she concludes she should sell in period 18. Continuing this way (a process known as backward induction), all sophisticated traders would end up selling the asset right at the start of the bubble when the price exceeds the fundamental, and a bubble would never emerge in the first place.

This conclusion requires that the sophisticated traders (or, at least, one third of them) are fully rational. Evidence from how people behave in real asset markets, or in experiments where they are asked to play a simple game like the one above, suggests that they do not draw out the implications of backward induction to their fullest. Rather, some are first-level reasoners, so they sell only after 20 periods after the bubble started. The second-level reasoners, as before, choose to sell after 19 periods, while the third-level reasoners realize this and conclude that they should attack after 18 periods. The process continues, leading to a distribution of traders wishing to sell at different times. The key for a fully rational trader is to predict how many first-, second-, third-, . . ., infinity-level reasoners are active in the marketplace. With this estimate at hand, she can figure out the optimal length of time riding the bubble.

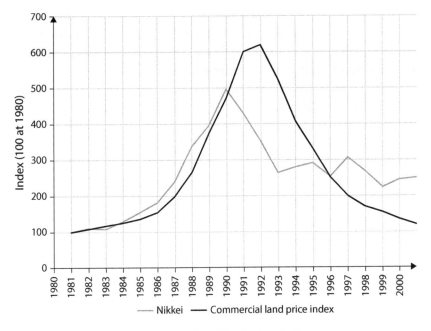

FIGURE 2.2. Stock and land prices in Japan

She wants to ride the bubble up to the period where finally the higher-level agents are more than 1/3 of the population. This allows the bubble to arise and persist.

When the attack actually happens depends both on the number of extrapolative agents and their impact on prices, as well as on the number of sophisticated agents at lower levels of reasoning. More of either leads the bubble to persist longer. Extrapolative expectations are a key driving force of the bubble that even very sophisticated traders will not overturn at first.

2.2   The Japanese Bubble of the Mid-1980s

In the late 1980s, Japan experienced a large stock market and real estate bubble, depicted in figure 2.2. Stock prices more than quadrupled, while commercial real estate prices increased more than sixfold in a span of 11 years. At its peak, the total land value in Japan was roughly 20% of the total wealth in the whole world. The land around the emperor's palace in Tokyo, which is about three quarters of a square mile, was estimated to be worth the same as all the land in California or Canada.

Arguably, the initial rise in stock and real estate values—the phase Minsky referred to as displacement—could be justified by changes in two fundamentals: a fall in interest rates and financial liberalization. In the mid 1980s, Japan was under international pressure to stimulate domestic demand in order to reduce its trade surplus, especially with the United States, whose current account deficit reached 3.5% of its GDP. Unwilling to expand government expenditures, Japan stimulated the economy by cutting the interest rate from 5% in January 1986 to 1% within a span of three years. These rate cuts in the 1980s took place against the backdrop of financial liberalization. Two examples are that people could now place bets on the exchange rate (via forward exchange contracts) without having a real transaction to justify them, and that some previous limit on short-run flows of capital (the yen conversion rule) were removed. In addition, large Japanese corporations could raise funds through equity warrant bonds, which were traded mainly in London. The combination of financial liberalization and lower interest rates boosted the fundamental value of real assets like stocks and real estate. This in turn led to expectations of ever rising stock and real estate markets. Extrapolative expectations took hold, and new investors entered the market inducing further price increases. The boom phase started with increased investments and GDP. But after the bubble popped, with a stock price collapse in 1991, decades of stagnation followed.[5]

2.3   The Internet Bubble of 1998–2000

In the late 1990s, the Internet boom led to a sharp rise in stock prices of technology companies. It was technological, not financial, innovation that drove the displacement phase of this bubble. Technological advancements, like the railroad booms in the 1830s and 1840s, can lead to excitement and overly optimistic expectations. For example, investors believed that many of the startup firms could become dominant in their markets and reap monopoly profits. While this might have been true for some firms, it was extrapolated to many. Another sign of the "irrational exuberance" was that firms that added the suffix .com to their name experienced a large jump in their stock value.

One feature that allowed the bubble to persist was that more sophisticated investors did not lean against this exuberance but preferred to "ride" the fast growing bubble.

Figure 2.3 documents that hedge funds, a sophisticated class of investors, were overexposed to technology stocks rather than acting as a price corrective

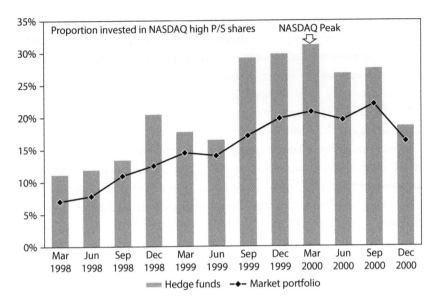

FIGURE 2.3. Hedge funds' holdings of technology stocks 1998–2000

force. Hedge fund portfolios were heavily tilted toward highly priced technology stocks compared to the average market portfolio. This overexposure peaked in September 1999, about six months before the peak of the technology bubble. Bubble riding was profitable insofar as hedge fund managers were able to predict some of the investor sentiment and exuberance. On a stock-by-stock basis, they started to cut back their holdings before prices collapsed, switching to technology stocks that still experienced rising prices. As a result, hedge fund managers captured the upturn, but avoided much of the downturn. There is another reason why fund managers, who manage others people's money, are particularly prone toward riding bubbles. Relative benchmarking makes not riding the bubble risky for them. If a fund manager were to lean against a growing bubble too early, he would underperform a benchmark index, and risk seeing investors leave the fund for its competitors. Underperforming fund managers have to scale their investment and unwind their positions, missing out on the rising prices.

The Internet bubble spurred innovative real investments, in fiber-optic cables, computers, and the like, as did investment in railroads in the booms of the 1830s and 1840s. New technologies often have to overcome important coordination problems. If firm A does not invest and switch its production process, then firm B has no incentive to change its process as well. Innovation bubbles are often accompanied by euphoria and cheap funding, which enable a fundamental technological transition to a new paradigm. This is in contrast to (non-investment) bubbles that are not technology driven, say real estate bubbles, which are not accompanied by lasting productivity gains.[6]

This time, the Internet stock market bubble did not end in a macro-financial crisis. The distinguishing feature of the Internet bubble was, in contrast, say, to the crash of 1929 that was followed by the Great Depression, that most stocks were bought outright and not debt-financed. Debt financing and leverage concentrates risk in the hands of a few and has adverse knock-on effects on the financial system and leads to larger dislocations in the real economy.[7] The aim of macroprudential regulation is to lean against credit-financed bubbles to reduce the likelihood that they emerge or persist. Leaning ex ante against the build-up of risk is more effective than cleaning up the fallout resulting from the bursting of a bubble. Since bubbles are often difficult to identify, policy often focuses on constraining the amount of credit and leverage that could be used to finance the bubble.

Notes

1. As mentioned in Kindleberger (1978).

2. For an introduction to models of trading due to different beliefs and how they can give rise to bubbles, see Scheinkman (2014). For discussions of many historical episodes of bubbles, see Garber (2000) and Quinn and Turner (2020).

3. Prices spiral down, often accelerated by margin calls and weakening balance sheets. If the run-up was financed with credit, amplification and spillover effects kick in, which can lead to severe overshooting also in the downturn.

4. "It is not a case of choosing those [faces] that, to the best of one's judgment, are really the prettiest, nor even those that average opinion genuinely thinks the prettiest. We have reached the third degree where we devote our intelligence to anticipating what average opinion expects the average opinion to be. And there are some, I believe, who practice the fourth, fifth and higher degrees."

5. This led the Bank of Japan to innovate many new policy instruments that are discussed in more detail in chapter 10.

6. The evidence in this section is based on Brunnermeier and Nagel (2004).

7. This will be the focus of chapter 5.

3

Capital Inflows and Their (Mis)allocation

BEFORE A crash, there is usually a prolonged time during which abundant credit sustains an investment boom. Sometimes this follows a liberalization of financial markets. Often, it is fueled by optimistic expectations by borrowers and lenders. Almost always, credit is cheap and plentiful, and financial markets grow to intermediate the large flow of capital from savers to borrowers.

Because poorer regions typically have more investment opportunities, and richer regions have more savers, capital tends to flow from developed to developing regions. Housing is often at the center of these flows since it is one of the largest risky assets available that is owned by many people, and because it can be easily used as collateral for borrowing. The increase in demand for construction and real estate services drives up economic activity and raises employment. A benevolent (and common) view of the run-up to a crisis focuses on the benefits from these large capital flows. They make financial markets become integrated, economies boom, and incomes converge across regions.

A modern view of capital flows focuses instead on how they are allocated across both sectors and firms. Poorer countries not only have fewer resources and more investment opportunities, but they are also worse at allocating capital to their most productive uses. Their financial markets, broadly defined as the markets that allocate capital across uses, are not deep enough. This is a result of both political interference, with myriad taxes, regulations, and corruption that favor some sectors and firms at the expense of others, as well as banks and financial markets, which are riddled with governance problems and are unsophisticated in evaluating projects. While sudden financial integration increases the capital stock, it also intensifies this misallocation. With abundant resources, bank managers become more lax at screening projects, and politicians are less eager to make structural reforms and enforce competition and smaller rents. Even if investment and production can boom, productivity falls.[1]

3.1   A Model of Misallocation

To understand how investment booms are tied to acute misallocation, consider a simple model. The economy has two sectors, and several firms in each of them, so that there is scope for two types of misallocation: between and within sectors. One sector, call it T for traded, produces goods that are traded in international markets subject to fierce competition—manufacturing being one good example. The other, call it N or non-traded, produces goods for the domestic market, which are protected from competition by natural and political barriers—construction and real estate being two suitable examples.

The economy has to allocate its scarce capital between the two sectors. The top panel of figure 3.1 shows the production possibilities frontier as a downward-sloping line: one more unit of output of good N must come with shifting some capital toward it, and so away from sector T, lowering the latter's output. Preferences for the two goods are represented by indifference curves that are convex to the origin. Ideally, the economy would operate at point A, where the highest utility is reached given the trade-off between resources.

Yet, sector N is protected by local interests. Politicians are sensitive to the number of voters that construction employs, to the visibility of public works and their electoral impact, and perhaps even to the eventual corruption that a close proximity between local politicians and local developers can engender. In turn, local bankers favor loans to construction projects, where collateral is available and easy to price. Large construction companies often have important shareholder stakes in local banks, pressuring the bank managers to favor them in allocating credit. Finally, construction and other non-tradable sectors, being protected from foreign competition, can more easily form local cartels and coordinate political contributions.

The mirror image of effectively subsidizing one sector is taxing another, since both change the relative rewards of deploying capital in one sector as opposed to the other. Therefore, firms in sector T now face a relative tax over their output, reducing their marginal product of capital after these taxes. The production frontier line is now flatter since diverting one unit of capital from the N to the T sector gives a lower return. This process of favoring sector N

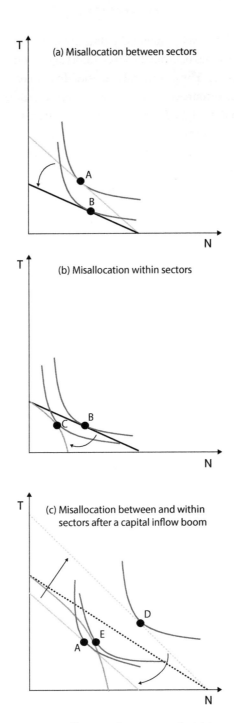

FIGURE 3.1. Misallocation between and within sectors

creates rents for those well connected politically who can capture the capital and collect the subsidies or avoid the taxes. Effort and resources are diverted to capturing those rents. These wasteful activities do not create any new output but directly lower resources for all in the economy, leading to a production frontier closer to the origin. For simplicity, the figure assumes that all of the taxes on sector T are lost this way, so the new frontier is a leftward rotation of the previous one. The new equilibrium, with misallocation between sectors, then occurs at point B.

In addition, there can be a misallocation within sector N, which is the focus of panel (b) of figure 3.1. Immune to foreign competition, this sector can more easily lobby for local regulations that restrict domestic competition. Sometimes, this takes the form of barriers preventing firms from growing too large. Politicians are receptive to the virtues of small firms because entrepreneurship is seen as a path to income mobility and because small firms employ a large share of the population. In addition, banks in underdeveloped financial markets lack the managerial talent and the tools to diversify their credit portfolios, so they are wary of giving large loans to a few firms. When this happens, it leads to within-sector misallocation, as the distribution of firm size becomes left-skewed, biased toward the smaller firms. In the other direction, especially in emerging economies, it is sometimes larger firms that receive special treatment. Politicians favor larger firms that have more political clout derived from employing many voters, and that have large contracts to provide essential government services. Financial markets favor larger firms because their owners may be major shareholders and directors of banks that channel credit to their non-financial businesses.

Taking the bias-to-small case (but symmetric arguments could be made with bias-to-large well-connected firms), consider a simple model where there is a limit on firm size of selling at most 1 unit of output. Imagine then that there are many potential firms to produce good N, and that the demand for this good is 3 units. One firm, the most productive, can produce all 3 units using 3 units of capital, as its productivity is 1. Yet, facing the upper bound, it can only produce 1 unit of output. The next best firm, which is less productive and if there was perfect competition would be out of business, finds itself with a demand to satisfy. It is only one third as productive, needing 3 units of capital as input to produce 1 unit of output. A third firm is able to operate, needing 5 units of capital to supply the last unit of output. In the end, the 3 units of output are produced using $1 + 3 + 5 = 9$ units of capital. Aggregate productivity is $3/9 = 1/3$, in contrast with the productivity of $3/3 = 1$ without the barriers to firm growth within the sector. A sign of this misallocation is the increase in the dispersion of productivity across firms in operation, as the market is prevented from driving the less productive ones out of business.

The middle panel of figure 3.1 shows the result of this misallocation within the sector. Each additional unit of good N is now produced with lower productivity, so that the distorted production frontier becomes concave to the origin since it takes more capital, and so less production of good T to get that extra unit of N. The economy operates at a point C, and welfare is lower.

The bottom panel of figure 3.1 combines these elements to show what happens after a sudden and large capital inflow. Absent the inefficiencies in an idealized world, capital flows would allow a shift from point A to point D. However, the abundance of resources worsens the misallocation between and within sectors and the economy ends up at point E instead. In the political sector, the pressure to reach agreements and make structural reforms is relaxed. In the financial sector, abundant credit that goes to many recipients makes it harder to distinguish the productive projects from those that are not. Another, third, reason why large capital inflows can worsen misallocation is that funds can get directed to assets with low supply elasticities, pushing up asset prices. This can generate capital gains, trigger extrapolative expectations, and thereby lead to asset price bubbles.[2] Bubbles relax collateral and financing constraints, spurring further credit to particular sectors, even if they are not particularly efficient, especially in the construction sector, as land is in fixed supply and is commonly used as collateral.

Before the inflow, the poor capital-scarce region may be in points similar to B and C in the middle panel, but the distance between these and the efficient point A in the top panel might be small. With more capital available, the economy expands. If this new capital were allocated efficiently through deep financial and political markets, the economy would move from point A to point D. Economic activity would be higher, and so would welfare. In this simple economy, productivity would be unchanged or may even rise as some of the capital is devoted to adopting new technologies.

With financial shallowness, the inflow of capital instead exacerbates the misallocation. The economy ends up in point E, very far from D, and potentially not far beyond point A. The economic boom is moderate or may barely even happen in spite of all the new capital flowing in. Aggregate productivity slumps and the dispersion of productivity rises, as the new capital is misallocated to more politically connected and less productive firms. Importantly, of course, the run-up of foreign funding will have to be repaid at some point in the future even as the economy is producing little, leading to problems that other chapters will explore.[3]

3.2   The Seeds of the Euro Crisis: Portugal's Twenty-First Century Slump

On January 1, 1999, twelve countries of the European Union adopted a common currency with a unit of account, the euro. Following the 1992 Maastricht Treaty, the goal was to deepen the single market for goods and services, and to create institutions that eliminated barriers to the free flow of capital across European regions. With the euro, the risk from exchange rates changing when sending capital abroad disappeared. The risk of sovereign default remained, as the Maastricht Treaty forbids European institutions from bailing out sovereigns in trouble, but optimistic investors seemed to ignore this as they were willing to lend to countries in the European periphery, with a history of default and fragile public finances, at quite low interest rates.

The combination of no exchange-rate risk and close to zero perceived default risk led to a large capital flow within the euro area. From the start of 2000 to the end of 2007, Germany and France ran a cumulative current account surplus (a measure of savings sent abroad) of €638 bn; Greece, Ireland, Portugal, and Spain had a matching cumulative current account deficit of €668 bn. As a whole, the euro area neither saved nor borrowed, but within it, the core regions sent vast amounts of capital to the periphery regions. For the periphery, this was a large flow: the GDP of the four countries in 2007 was a mere €1,635 bn, and their external debt by then had risen to €5,507 bn.

Capital markets and political institutions in the periphery lacked the depth to channel these large flows of capital. Construction and wholesale trade sectors boomed at the expense of tradable sectors, even though productivity growth was higher in the latter and stagnated in the former. The dispersion of productivity within sectors continuously rose from the start of the euro, just as Total Factor Productivity (TFP, a measure of the economy's total productive efficiency, capturing the amount of output in excess of inputs used in production) stagnated in all of the periphery countries. GDP grew due to additional labor and capital inputs rather than productivity improvements. Indeed, productivity might have declined as economic activity shifted from more productive to less productive sectors and to less productive firms within a sector.

Figure 3.2 illustrates these common facts across the periphery region for the case of Portugal. The figure plots actual TFP growth before and after the

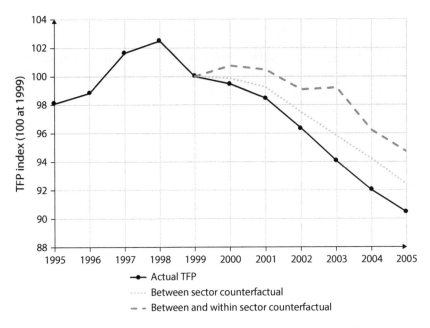

FIGURE 3.2. Actual and counterfactual TFP in Portugal

euro, showing the slump that coincided with the euro. Also in the figure are two counterfactual measures that separate the effects of misallocation. The first counterfactual TFP keeps the relative size of each economic sector at its 1999 level. The sectors that expanded were those that were relatively less productive. The second counterfactual shows productivity if the misallocation within sectors had stayed at its 1999 levels as well. In the sectors that grew, productivity fell. Both combined, misallocation partly accounts for the surprising Portuguese productivity slump at the start of the century.

This allocation of capital and fall in productivity has implications for international competitiveness. The misallocation of capital spills over to labor by raising the wages of workers in the construction and public-service sectors. With abundant capital, non-tradable sectors pay higher wages and attract more workers. In Portugal, the average earnings of construction and public-sector workers relative to manufacturing workers increased significantly. This raised the costs of firms in tradable sectors, so that the competitiveness of Portuguese firms fell, and trade deficits resulted. Between 2000 and 2007, the Portuguese real exchange rate, a measure of the price of Portuguese goods vis-a-vis foreign goods, appreciated by 12%. The cumulative trade deficit of the country between 2000 and 2007 was 47% of 2007's GDP.[4]

3.3 Chile's 1970s Liberalization and 1982 Crash

In September 1973, Augusto Pinochet rose to power in Chile through a military coup. He implemented a program of financial liberalization, aimed at ending the repression of the previous three years of socialist economic planning, which had included strict credit rationing, sharply negative real interest rates for depositors, and a fully state-owned financial sector. In 1974, most banks were privatized, and for the next few years, the restrictions on their operations were removed, including on foreign borrowing. There was little financial supervision, interest rates were set freely, with no limits on credit, no minimal reserves that banks had to hold at the central bank, and no public guarantee of deposits, as well as an explicit commitment by the government to not bail out banks. This laissez-faire did not last long: in January 1977, a large bank (Banco Osorno) failed, its depositors were rescued, and between then and 1980 the government introduced requirements that banks had to hold a minimum amount of capital and hold 10% of their deposits at the central bank.

At the same time, on the macroeconomic front, the government gradually reduced trade barriers after 1973 down to a uniform tariff of only 10% by 1979, and removed restrictions to the flow of capital. In 1979, the Chilean peso was pegged to the U.S. dollar. As in the periphery of Europe with the euro, the removal of exchange rate risk and other barriers to capital flows led to large inflows of capital: by 1981, the current account deficit was 14% of GDP. The financial system boomed, intermediating these flows, and total financial assets rose from 16% of GDP in 1973 to 39% in 1981. Between 1977 and 1981, the real size of loan portfolios increased by a factor of approximately 6.

One feature of the Chilean business sector, common in many emerging economies, was the existence of large business conglomerates with a diverse group of companies. With financial liberalization, they expanded and included at least one of the recently privatized banks. The government sold these often on favorable terms to their previous owners or to people close to the political regime, who then used the bank credit to buy industrial firms in further privatizations and grow the group. During the transition period of 1977–80, these groups were the only ones that had access to private foreign borrowing at low interest rates through their banks, and could then invest these domestically, earning high returns in the sector that benefitted from the reduction in tariff rates. They favored using their abundant capital within the group, even if it is invested in sectors and firms with small returns. In 1979, 80% of Chilean bank capital was concentrated in these groups, and as they grew, their ability

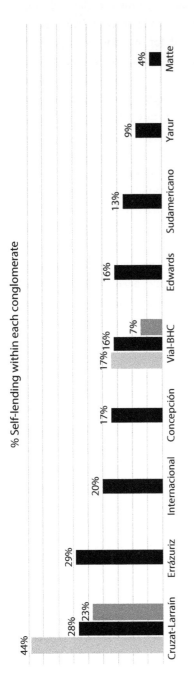

% Self-lending within each conglomerate

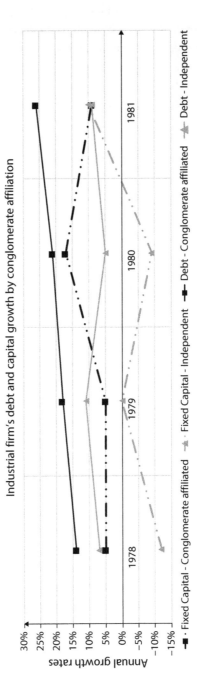

Industrial firm's debt and capital growth by conglomerate affiliation

FIGURE 3.3. The Chilean business groups of 1976–82

Note: Each label in the top panel refers to a separate conglomerate. Each bar refers to the % of total credit given by a bank in the group (there can be as many as three) to companies within the conglomerate.

to misallocate capital within the group and away from their most efficient use was even higher.

The top panel in figure 3.3 shows, for each conglomerate, the high fraction of credit given by each of the banks in the conglomerate (three banks for two of the conglomerates, and just one bank for the other seven). Those companies borrowed heavily. The banks of the same group allocated credit preferentially to the businesses within the conglomerate, whether those were the most productive uses of the capital or not. Capital was arguably misallocated within industries, toward firms that belonged to groups. The bottom panel shows how during this period, bank credit and capital accumulation were much higher for companies within a group.

With high debt comes the risk of rising interest rates. The peg to the U.S. dollar implied importing the tight U.S. monetary policy of the early 1980s, as well as an appreciation relative to Chile's trading partners that lowered competitiveness. Capital flows reversed, away from Chile, and real interest rates rose to 40% by the end of 1981. In 1982, the peg of the peso was dropped and it devalued by almost half. In November 1981, eight financial institutions were rescued by the government, and in January 1983, five needed a large government intervention, three were liquidated, and two became directly supervised. By the end of 1983, the government owned more than 50% of the banking system. The businesses within the groups suffered, and in June 1982, the supervisory authorities forbade the banks from continuing to roll over loans to them, with large unrealized losses, drastically limiting the self-lending within the business groups. GNP fell by 14% in 1982, and there were more than 800 company bankruptcies. Unemployment reached 30% in 1983.

The crisis laid bare the misallocation of resources within the Chilean economy. As it almost always happens in a crisis, productivity fell further. Yet, in spite of the 10% decline in total factor productivity in the manufacturing sector, within-industry allocative efficiency barely improved. Removing the preferential treatment of the inefficient firms affiliated with the groups partly offset the disruption brought by the deep crisis. Argentina and Uruguay went through similar crises at the time, with similar diagnoses as Chile.[5]

Notes

1. The bubbles in chapter 2 are themselves a form of misallocation. As people plunge into the bubble, they divert their wealth away from more productive uses. This is especially noticeable in cases, like the Japanese or the U.S. ones that we discussed, where the bubbles are in land or

housing. When this happens, resources get drawn into construction of new structures. Finally, and a complementary channel, the desire to ride the bubble may be one of the reasons behind the capital inflows in the first place.

2. As explained in chapter 2.

3. Diaz-Alejandro (1985) is the early classic on the misallocation hypothesis applied to Chile, while Reis (2013) is the modern statement of the misallocation theory of slumps and crashes behind the euro crisis. Fernández-Villaverde, Garicano, and Santos (2013) elaborate on how politics and finance interact to cause the misallocation in the first place.

4. For the data and discussion of the Portuguese episode, see Reis (2013) and Dias, Marques, and Richmond (2016). For follow-up empirical applications to Spain instead, see Gopinath et al. (2017) and Castillo-Martinez (2020).

5. For more on the evolution in Chile and the data that we use, see de la Cuadra and Valdés (1990), Galvez and Tybout (1985), and Arellano (1985).

4

Banks and Their Cousins

IN THE traditional view of a bank, its balance sheet is simple. On the asset side are holdings of mortgages and business loans, as well as some financial assets, mostly government bonds. By holding and pooling many assets, banks take advantage of the fact that asset prices do not co-move perfectly. Risk is reduced as some asset prices move up at the same time as others move down. Banks also perform the important role of selecting and monitoring domestic borrowers in order to reduce the chances of default. Monitoring takes effort that the banker would rather not make, so she must have some skin in the game in the form of an adequate amount of equity, which will fall in value if the loans are not repaid. This way, the banker will want to put effort into monitoring and will avoid taking too many risks with the funds of the depositors.

Banks perform another useful role: transforming maturity and liquidity, from illiquid long-term assets to liquid short-term liabilities. Their assets are typically long-term and have little market liquidity, since they cannot be easily sold. In contrast, the banks' liabilities, made up of demand deposits, are short-term and can be withdrawn at a moment's notice. This allows depositors to have access to funds when they need them, while at the same time the bank uses their pooled funds to finance long-term investments. This transformation leaves banks exposed to runs. If all the depositors were to demand to have their deposits redeemed at the same time, the bank would not be able to call in its loans and sell its assets to honor its promises. Moreover, if one depositor expects the others to run to the bank, she will want to run as well to try to be ahead in the line and to be able to withdraw funds before they run out. Policy, in the form of deposit insurance backed by fiscal authorities, or lender of last resort by monetary authorities, can eliminate the incentive for depositors to run, thus preserving the bank's socially beneficial role of transforming maturity. If depositors know that their deposits will always be honored, they no longer need to run. Combined with inertia by households, this policy has been successful at making demand deposits a relatively stable funding source for banks.

The flow of capital across countries rarely happens directly between households and corporations, nor through a single bank across the two countries. Rather, it is intermediated by financial markets and institutions, as savers in core regions deposit their savings in banks there, and these banks proceed to lend them to banks in the periphery. Moreover, the modern financial system has changed over the previous decades, and looks different from the description above. Modern banks are different in ways that are prone to financial crises when intermediating large capital flows.[1]

4.1   Modern and Shadow Banks

On the asset side, modern banks securitize a significant share of their loans, especially mortgages. This involves combining them in a pool to remove the idiosyncratic risk, and selling the future revenue stream that comes from the total payments of the mortgages, in exchange for a payment today. Previously hard-to-trade mortgages become, at least apparently, tradable securities. As a result, in the balance sheet of a modern bank, the share of traded assets, whose value is assessed using current market prices, is considerably larger than that of a traditional bank. This marking-to-market of assets makes banks' balance sheets more transparent but also more volatile. When prices are rising, in the run-up to a crisis, it boosts balance sheets even when these capital gains are about to disappear when asset prices revert. Even outside of crashes, price overreactions during market up- and downturns exacerbate bank gains and losses, as the risk may leave one individual bank's balance sheet, but stays primarily within the banking system, as other banks would buy the securities or extend loans to others taking these securities as collateral.

On the liability side, modern banks rely on a new source of funding beyond deposits and shareholder equity: the wholesale funding market. Instead of borrowing from households, funding is obtained from other financial institutions, mostly through two vehicles. The first is short-term borrowing in the unsecured interbank market (so without collateral). Unlike depositors, other financial institutions are well informed and quick to withdraw their loans, well before depositors run. Inertia can no longer be counted on to prevent runs, and their ability to suspend funding before depositors gives financial institutions effective seniority.[2]

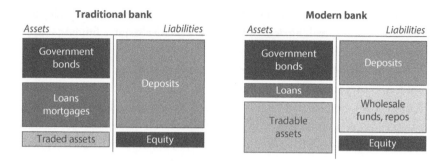

FIGURE 4.1. Traditional and modern banks' balance sheets

The second source of wholesale funding is repurchase agreements, or repos, where securities are temporarily sold to other financial institutions to be later repurchased at a pre-agreed price. These repos have three features that have important implications for banks' funding features. First, a security is sold in a repo transaction for a price below its market value, the difference being a haircut (or margin) that the borrower retains as a safety cushion for the case that the value of the collateral changes. Banks therefore are exposed to a new funding risk: that haircuts are suddenly raised. Second, repos typically have short durations and must be rolled over frequently, so they can quickly disappear as a source of funding. Finally, because repos are collateralized borrowing, lenders can collect that collateral if the bank fails, regardless of the other credits on the bank. As a result, repos enjoy seniority over demand deposit holders and unsecured interbank loans. As a consequence, interbank funding becomes more fickle and risk is pushed onto deposit holders or deposit insurance facilities.

Figure 4.1 contrasts the composition of the balance sheets of traditional and modern banks. Assets and liabilities interact as banks securitize loans to transform them into tradable assets, and then use these as collateral to obtain repo funding, allowing them to give out more loans. As such, modern banks are able to grow rapidly. Wholesale funding can be obtained more quickly than deposits can be collected. Borrowing from financial markets can be done overnight, while raising deposits requires a slow and costly process of opening branches and attracting customers. Creditors are willing to fund these quick expansions of banks protected by their effective seniority, and by the collateral given by repos. Because wholesale markets work across borders, fragmented regulation across multiple jurisdictions struggles to keep this growth in check.

Modern banks are riskier than traditional banks on three accounts. First, because they grow quickly supported on wholesale borrowing, the share of their net worth that funds the assets and provides skin in the game is lower. Thus, the incentives for banks to exert effort to monitor the quality of their loans and to be prudent when taking on risk become weaker.

Second, funding liquidity risk is higher. Unlike deposit retail funding, wholesale funding can be fickle since the lenders are quick to exit at the first sign of trouble. More generally, some institutions do not take deposits at all, so they avoid the government regulation that comes with them, funding themselves entirely through wholesale funding. They continue to use short-term funding to make long-term investments, so they are prone to bank runs, but they do not benefit from any government insurance on their funding. Mutual funds, bond funds, and others form a "shadow banking" sector with modern features.

Third, modern banks amplify asset-price cycles. When the price of houses (or other collateral) rises, the marked-to-market assets on banks' balance sheets increase right away. This increase in the value of collateral makes it easier to obtain wholesale funding in the repo market. This in turn allows for further lending by banks, lowers the cost of mortgages, increases the demand for houses, and therefore leads to further appreciation.[3]

Modern banking requires changes in regulation. A first change is to include modern shadow banks, as they are exposed to the same dangers. Second, because of funding liquidity risk and amplification of asset prices, regulators must complement the assessment of the risk of each individual financial institution in isolation with a macro-wide perspective. This macroprudential regulation takes into account the spillovers across financial institutions and to the macro economy. Third, regulation has to be dynamic, tight when prices are rising and relaxed after they crash.

4.2   U.S. Subprime Mortgages and Securitization

Few financial innovations exemplified the shift toward modern banks and shadow banks more than the securitization wave in the United States during the run-up prior to the global financial crisis of 2007–08. Mortgage and other lending was fundamentally transformed in the decade before the crisis. The rise of securitized products led to a flood of cheap credit, to lower lending standards, and ultimately to an increase of house prices.

After banks granted loans and mortgages, they repacked them in so-called "structured" products, also referred to as collateralized debt obligations

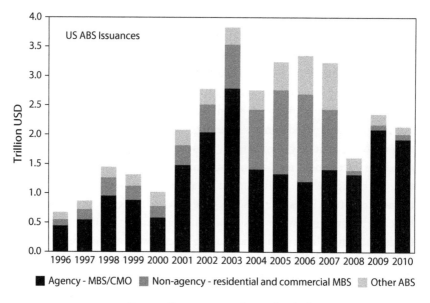

FIGURE 4.2. Issues of mortgage and asset-backed securities

(CDOs). If the underlying assets were auto loans, credit card receivables, and other assets, they were generally referred to as asset-backed securities (ABS). The pool of these loans was sliced into different tranches, where the cash flows from the underlying assets first pay off the senior tranche and the left-over cash flows go to the junior tranches, which are therefore riskier. Money market funds, European banks, and other institutional investors were eager to buy the senior tranches. How risky a senior tranche is depends on the diversification benefits across the underlying loans in the pool. If they are highly positively correlated—in an extreme, if all mortgages default at the same time and default completely, their payoff drops to zero—the senior tranche is just as risky as the original loans. The statistical models that were used to evaluate the riskiness of the tranches at the time underestimated the default correlations across mortgages. They relied too much on the recent U.S. history, during which house price downturns were regional, not national, phenomena.

Mortgages in the United States were securitized by private banks, but also by semi-private government sponsored enterprises, GSE agencies. One of them, Ginnie Mae, issued bonds which enjoyed explicit government guarantees, while the other two main ones, Fannie Mae and Freddie Mac, issued bonds that only had an implicit government guarantee. Figure 4.2 shows the expansion of mortgage-backed securities across these different types, also adding asset-backed securities, which were dominated by short-term paper backed by auto loans and credit card receivables.

In spite of increasing doubts that the run-up in the housing market was unsustainable, the financial sector kept on securitizing mortgages and other loans. Citigroup's former CEO, Chuck Prince, famously summed up the attitude on Wall Street in July 2007 by referring to Keynes' analogy between bubbles and musical chairs. "When the music stops, in terms of liquidity, things will be complicated. But as long as the music is playing, you've got to get up and dance. We're still dancing."

The music started to stop soon afterward. Several European banks, which held these tranches, faced difficulties. In March 2008 the investment bank Bear Stearns failed, and in July the U.S. government gave an explicit guarantee to Fannie Mae and Freddie Mac and put them in conservatorship. When Lehman Brothers declared bankruptcy in September 2008, it triggered a global financial crisis, and most U.S. banks (including Citigroup) as well as other institutions (for example, AIG, a large insurance company) were kept afloat only by using public bailout funds.

4.3   The Spanish Credit Boom of the 2000s

Banks were at the center of the capital flows in the euro area. Measures of the claims of core banks on periphery banks closely match the evolution of capital flows in the 2000–07 period. In turn, these capital flows were almost entirely accounted for by interbank debt, as there was little equity or physical property that exchanged hands.

A rough account of the cross-border flows of capital in the lead-up to the euro crisis is as follows. Savers in the core regions made short-term deposits in core financial institutions. These institutions sent the capital through the wholesale market as short-term loans to periphery financial institutions. The periphery banks lent funds to projects, privileging sectors like housing, that have tangible collateral, and which are easy to securitize and sell in deep markets, allowing the banks to expand quickly.[4] Part of these loans were used to pay for wages in the periphery, which were then used to pay for imports of intermediate inputs from the more productive and competitive core countries. Firms in the core countries deposited their receipts from the sales to the periphery in the core banks, completing the cycle. Through this cycle, the modern banks in the periphery relying on short-term funding grew quickly, providing loans that spurred the misallocation between sectors and further enhancing the capital flows (or current account imbalances) across borders.

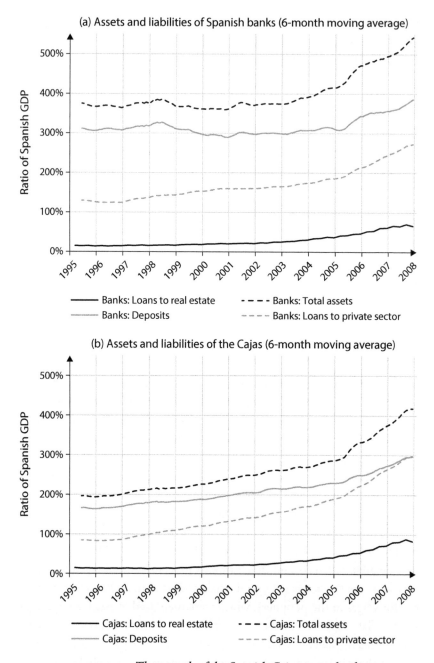

FIGURE 4.3. The growth of the Spanish Cajas versus banks

Figure 4.3 illustrates this phenomenon for the Spanish banking sector by plotting data from the balance sheet of Spanish banks as a ratio of GDP. The figure separates traditional banks and local savings and loan banks, the "Cajas," which had traditionally been small banks, with strong ties to local politicians, specialized in holding mortgages in their regions. Starting around 2002, the Spanish banking sector started expanding at a rapid rate. For the Cajas, this growth happened in spite of little growth in deposits. The new ability to securitize and sell their mortgages, and to have access to the wholesale market, allowed the Cajas to become modern banks and grow quickly. With this, they were able to fund an increase in credit to real estate, at a significantly faster rate than that of the other banks. By 2007, the Cajas accounted for 52% of all loans to the private sector in Spain, and their loans to the real estate sector had increased by a factor of 4.9. Ten years later, all of the Cajas had been dismantled or absorbed by other banks as a result of their high losses and mismanagement.

European banks have three distinctive features relative to U.S. banks. First, the size of bank credit relative to total GDP is significantly larger in Europe (and in Asia) than in the United States. On the other side of the Atlantic, the corporate bond market is roughly equally important as a source of funds to firms, whereas bank financing is dominant in Europe. Second, the largest few banks in each European country are very large relative to their countries, with total assets often in excess of annual GDP. If a bank makes large losses, its national host country has to solve the problem of bailing it out or compensating depositors. But European banks are so large that any individual country would have trouble doing so. Third, the flows of capital happen across multiple regions in Europe, involving countries with different deposit insurance mechanisms, different resolution authorities for troubled banks, and different fiscal authorities and legal systems behind these. These did not combine to serve as a substitute to the roles that deposit insurance and lender of last resort play in traditional banking. Altogether, the advent of rapidly growing modern banks implied that banking sector problems would have a larger impact on the European economy, and at the same time the sovereign safety net of the financial sector was unreliable.[5]

Notes

1. Aside from their role in transforming maturity, banks perform other roles that intersect with the previous chapters. For one, banks often lend to optimists and speculators riding the bubbles discussed in chapter 2. Also, banks are often key culprits in the misallocation of capital,

as we discussed at length in chapter 3. The classic reference for banks' maturity mismatch and runs is Diamond and Dybvig (1983).

2. For empirical evidence see Blickle, Brunnermeier, and Luck (2019).

3. See Brunnermeier (2009), Admati and Hellwig (2014), and Gorton (2010) for a discussion of modern banks and their funding.

4. This provided a new dimension of misallocation beyond the one described in the chapter 3.

5. Santos (2017) presents a thorough discussion of the Spanish banking sector. Gorton and Tallman (2018) provide many more historical episodes where similar dynamics were at play.

PART II

Crashes: Triggers and Amplifiers

5

Systemic Risk, Amplification, and Contagion

THE PREVIOUS section of this book discussed the buildup to a macro-financial crisis. At the outset of the crisis, one often finds financial institutions that are funding themselves with short-term debt to other financial institutions that is tied to collateral from securitizing its investments. These banks allocate capital to investments in the real economy that can be biased toward non-tradable sectors and projects of a certain size, even if these have inferior returns. The prices in financial markets may seem to be much above fundamental value, and yet speculators continue to ride the bubble.

In this context, an abrupt decline in the price of a financial asset that is not even that widely held, the default in loans to a real investment project that threatens only a few banks, or a run on the funding of an individual bank may each seem harmless at first. Yet, this chapter discusses how a financial system that has the aforementioned ingredients can greatly amplify these shocks. Modern banks that are connected through financial markets want to mimic each other's actions, so when some sell an asset, others want to sell the same asset as well, and when some cut credit to some sectors, others withhold loans to the same sectors. This creates adverse feedback loops that amplify initial exogenous triggers. If these amplifying forces are strong enough, there may be multiple equilibria, so that even just a switch to more pessimism by financial institutions can trigger a crisis. The system self-generates systemic risk.[1]

5.1 Strategic Complementarities, Amplification, Multiplicity

Modern financial markets depend critically on how each individual market participant reacts to the behavior of others. It is this herd behavior together with spillover effects that constitutes systemic risk. Figure 5.1 presents a graphical model of these interactions. On the vertical axis is the choice of how much to lend by an individual bank, and on the horizontal axis is the lending of other banks. More generally, the diagram represents the actions by participants in financial markets, whether these are choices to hold an asset or to roll over a repo. The curves give the best response of a bank to the others' actions: how much it will choose to lend given the others' behavior.

If the best response function slopes downward, as in the top panel, then the bank's incentives or constraints would be such that it decreases lending whenever others increase their average lending. In game theory terms, actions are said to be strategic substitutes. This may have been an adequate description of traditional financial markets. When other bank expands credit, there are fewer good projects looking for financing, so a traditional bank's response is to cut loans. Or, when more loans to buy a house are given out, this raises the price of houses, so that fewer further borrowers find it desirable to ask for credit from a bank.

Other banks in the market face the same problem. Each of them has its own best response function. A Nash equilibrium happens when each bank is doing what is best given what others are doing, and so they are all on their best responses. We assume, for simplicity, that all banks are identical. Therefore, the best response of the other banks is the symmetric version of the best response of the individual bank in the figure, and the equilibrium happens where the curve crosses the 45 degree line. Since every bank is the same in our illustration, in the equilibrium every single individual one chooses to do what the group of all others is also doing.

Because the best response slopes downward, the system is stable in two senses. First, there is a unique equilibrium at point O. Second, shifts in the best response function lead to moderate changes in this equilibrium. When the best response shifts down to the dashed curve, perhaps because banks become better aware of risks, or investors have fewer funds to buy assets with, the individual bank wants to cut lending (down arrow). As other banks cut their lending as well (left arrow), the individual bank now wants to respond by raising lending (up arrow). As the other banks raise lending, the individual bank now wants to cut, and so on in a cobweb process that leads to a new equilibrium at point H. As the figure shows, the initial shock is attenuated by the strategic interaction between the banks.

With a modern banking system, we have instead the situation in the bottom panel of the figure. When other banks cut lending and this lowers the price of

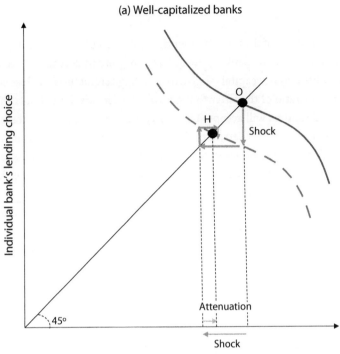

(a) Well-capitalized banks

Individual bank's lending choice

O

H

Shock

45°

Attenuation

Shock

All other banks' lending choice

(b) Banks with excessive leverage

Individual bank's lending choice

O

H

Shock

L

D

45°

Multiplicity   Amplification

Shock

All other banks' lending choice

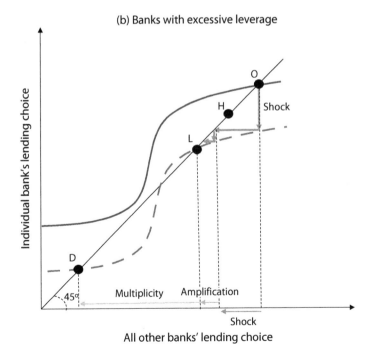

FIGURE 5.1. Amplification and multiplicity

housing, the value of these traded securities, like that of securitized mortgages, falls. Because modern banks grow quickly, they are undercapitalized, in that they have little equity capital relative to their large credit funding. Hence, their leverage (the ratio of the latter to the former) is already at the limits that regulators and funders will accept. Therefore, they cannot take advantage of the low asset prices to buy assets, as traditional well-capitalized banks can. Instead, as a bank's own tradable assets fall in price, its equity value tanks. Its leverage ratio increases, so the undercapitalized bank must shrink its balance sheet by shedding assets, exactly when asset values are low.[2]

When the entire financial sector is trying to sell assets at the same time, there is little market liquidity. That is, it is hard to sell the assets, or to redeploy them to other uses. This leads to fire sales, a situation when many must sell at any price and so the price has to fall considerably before demand meets supply again. Because each bank anticipates that all other banks will be shedding their assets, each will have an incentive to be the first one to sell, so asset prices fall quickly.

Low asset prices then reduce the banks' funding liquidity, understood as their ability to roll over their funds from creditors. The lack of funding makes it more difficult for banks to keep their assets. In part, this happens because of a loss spiral: the fall in the collateral value of assets leads to cuts in funding, for a fixed margin. In addition a margin spiral can emerge: as collateral values fall, lenders raise the margins in anticipation of the fire sale drop in prices. A collateral asset worth €100 can now be used to raise only €80 instead of €95 as before, so again banks' borrowing must be lower.

These two funding liquidity spirals combine to make the best response curves slope upward, represented by the curve in the bottom panel. When average actions of others increase, the participant chooses a more aggressive action. The actions of the banks are now strategic complements.

The change from well-capitalized and regulated banks to banks with excessive (hidden) leverage, that is, from the top to the bottom panel, or from downward-sloping to upward-sloping best response curves, would not be immediately apparent. The initial equilibrium would be at point O in both cases. But the system is now unstable in two ways after a shock that shifts the best response curve down. First, the same shock that shifts the curve by the same vertical distance, now leads instead to a change in actions captured by the equilibrium at point L. After the initial cut of the individual bank, others cut as well, and the former wants to cut more.

Whereas before the initial individual cut led to an attenuating rise in reaction to others toward the new equilibrium, now it leads to an amplification of the initial shock. When house prices fall, one bank's collateral is worth less, it has to repay some of its funding, and so it lends less. But as it lends less, house prices fall more making other banks also suffer losses and forcing them to lend less as well. In the end, the fall in lending and in house prices gets amplified from the initial shock to point L.

Second, there may be a new (stable) equilibrium indicated by the bottom-left D point. If people simply stop believing in the outcome with high lending, and think that all others will lend less, this is sufficient to lead to an outcome with less lending instantly materializing. There is multiplicity of equilibria. If each bank anticipates that others will cut lending, it anticipates the resulting fire sales and price drops, as well as the losses spiral and margins spiral. It will cut lending beforehand, triggering the depressed-lending equilibrium.

To conclude, after an adverse shock, three outcomes are possible. With traditional, well-capitalized banks that hold few traded assets and little collateralized borrowing subject to margins that must be rolled over all the time, the financial market ends up in the top-right H equilibrium after a shock to lending, as well as to asset prices or bank capital. But with highly leveraged (shadow) banks, fire sales and liquidity spirals amplify the shock via a system-wide fire sale and deleveraging, and the financial market moves to the middle low-lending L equilibrium. In the worst case, the economy can jump to the bottom-left D equilibrium, where volatility and margins are high due to a shift in beliefs, and lending is depressed.

These new outcomes are due to strategic complementarity between banks. A related, but distinct, concept is that of pecuniary externalities. When some banks sell assets, this pushes their prices down. Because other banks hold some of these assets and use them as collateral, the fall in price means that they realize losses and that their collateral constraints become tighter. The actions of the first banks cause losses to the other banks—an externality. An externality is distinct from a strategic complementarity, which is about the other banks' reaction, i.e., responding by selling assets as well. Strategic complementarities lead to amplification and multiplicity. All effects are larger, including the externalities. Together they lead to large systemic risk since losses in some financial institutions spill over to losses across the whole financial system.

5.2   Systemic Risk in the Irish Banking Sector in the 2000s

In the summer of 2007, news of bad loans in the U.S. subprime market triggered losses in the American investments of some European banks, especially in the core regions. This led these banks to cut back their interbank lending as

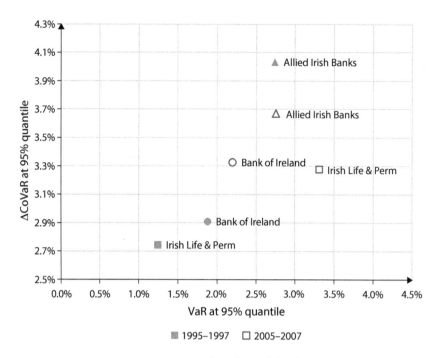

FIGURE 5.2. Systemic risk in the Irish banking sector

well as their repo purchases of securitized mortgages issued by the periphery countries' banks. At the same time, U.S. money market funds, which had been rolling over repos to European banks for years, withdrew from this market between 2007 and 2008 as a result of the growing U.S. financial crisis. Combined, these two forces led to a negative shock to the supply of bank funding in the wholesale market.

Irish banks were particularly reliant on this foreign wholesale funding, and had also invested in American securities. Over the previous decade, they had transitioned from traditional to modern banks, and had correspondingly grown significantly, providing plentiful credit to the housing sector. The negative shock to the funds available triggered fire sales and liquidity spirals that led to a large fall in lending and in house prices. The large losses spilled over to each other, leading to a systemic banking crisis and a deep recession in Ireland.

Figure 5.2 measures the systemic nature of the Irish banking sector as it moved from traditional to modern banking. On the horizontal axis is a measure of how individually risky a bank is, expressed in terms of the size of the losses in the value of its equity in the worst 5% of the weeks during a two-year period. This is known as value-at-risk (VaR) and it measures the risk of particular bank in isolation, the focus of microprudential regulation. On the vertical axis is a measure of systemic risk, computed by calculating how much the value at risk of the banking sector at large changes conditional on one particular bank's being under distress. This systemic risk measure is called ΔCoVaR. It measures how much the distress of a particular single bank spills over to the banking sector and is at the core of macroprudential regulation. The three filled symbols in the figure show these two measures for each of the three major Irish banks in the 1995–97 period.

In the ten years that followed, Irish banks transitioned from being traditional to modern banks. Their growth, concentrated in the real estate sector, led to an increase in their risk. For two of the three banks, VaR increased and systemic risk measured by ΔCoVaR increased with it, significantly so. When the financial shock arrived from abroad, the strategic complementarities amplified it so much that credit to private enterprises in the construction and real estate sectors fell an astounding 48% between the middle of 2008 and the end of 2010. Accompanying it was a propagation to the real economy reflected in a fall in residential property prices in Dublin of a record 35%. The systemic risk captured in the estimates in figure 5.2 revealed itself, and by the start of 2009 the private equity of all three banks had been almost entirely wiped out.

Faced with a systemic crisis, policymakers want to intervene to attenuate the amplification of the shocks to the real economy. This can be justified if the externalities involved are large. One way to stop the funding spirals is for the central bank to lend to banks. Yet, central bank lending requires the banks to have collateral, typically in the form of government bonds. Another is for governments to bail out banks through loans or recapitalizations that more or less explicitly nationalize the banks. Recapitalizations require trusting that, unlike the typical failing business, the banks remain economically solvent. Both were done in Ireland. A third policy intervention, aimed at preventing the jump in equilibrium due to multiplicity, is to conduct public stress tests of banks' balance sheets so as to make it known to each individual bank that the other banks will not be compelled to cut their lending in the near future. This was done in Europe, although with limited success, unlike in the United States, where it seemed to be particularly effective.[3]

5.3   The Emerging Markets' Storm of 1997–98

Strategic complementarities not only amplify shocks within one financial system, but also propagate them across borders through multiple channels. First, banks that lend internationally, typically do so to many countries. When one country has trouble repaying, the losses of the banks may lead them to cut credit to others. Second, when one country's currency sharply loses value, investors in nearby countries that had assets in that country suffer large losses in terms of their domestic currency. Third, the depreciation of the currency implies that the terms of trade of its main trading partners worsen, significantly putting strain on its export sector. Finally, when one country's sovereign bonds abruptly lose value, the funds that invest in its markets face margin calls, and must selloff their bond holdings in other countries. Through bank credit, foreign direct investment, trade, or investment funds, the forces explained in this chapter come to play.

A striking example of these forces was the global crisis of 1997–98. Throughout the 1990s, the financial sector in South East Asian countries started to develop the features of modern banking that generate strategic complementarities. Short-term foreign borrowing had boomed, through domestic banks, and was often denominated in foreign currency. This fueled large increases in domestic credit. Some of it went to business projects, sometimes with poor returns, and much went to real estate, leading to increases in house prices, rising collateral values, and further lending. At the same time, after large growth in the previous decade, exports slowed, a major export market (Japan) stagnated, and current account deficits widened.

The year of 1996 came with several adverse shocks: terms of trade deteriorated, real estate and stock markets in the region fell in value, and the U.S. dollar, to which many countries in the region were pegged, sharply appreciated relative to the euro or the yen, hurting competitiveness, and leading to a speculative attack on the Thai baht in November and December of that year. These correspond to a shift in the best response in the model. Wide losses and some outright defaults started to emerge in the corporate and financial sectors. Thailand offers a good example of the amplification of this shock. At the end of 1996, it had a current account deficit of 8.5% of GDP, and a significant slowdown of real growth. After a company (Somprasong) missed payments on foreign debt in February 1997, the government recognized that some property loans would not be paid back. One financial company (Finance One) had large losses, and the government forced it to merge with another in May. With its reserves of foreign currency depleted, on July 2, the central bank floated the baht, which depreciated by 20% within one month.

Figure 5.3 shows that the interest rates on Thai government bonds, which had been rising throughout the year, spiked at this time, as investors expected

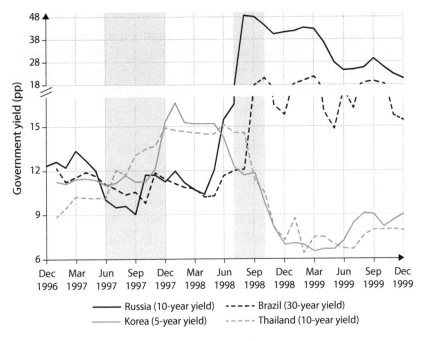

FIGURE 5.3. Government long-term yields during the Asian crisis

negative returns from further depreciation or outright default given the fragile state of government finances. Throughout the year, net capital outflows were $14 bn. This shock propagated through the region, as interest rates in Malaysia, Indonesia, and the Philippines followed a similar path. They had similar problems as Thailand, and once the baht depreciated, their currencies came under intense speculative attacks.

The events that followed a few months later suggest that there might have been a shift between two equilibria. Nearby Korea had limited trade linkages to Thailand and the other countries in crisis. It did, though, share with them its main creditors, Japanese and European commercial banks. These cut lending and, in October 1997, the Korean won suddenly came under attack as foreign investors ran to take their capital out of the country. The central bank let the won depreciate gradually with respect to the dollar by 8% that month but the sales continued, and the price of the currency and of Korean assets fell by another 25%, and by 4% in a single week in December. A fall in government bond prices, as all run to sell them, is equivalent to a spike in their yields. The 1997 sell-off of Korean bonds is visible in figure 5.3. Similar events took place in Indonesia and, to a smaller extent, in Singapore and Hong Kong.

Two features of these crises in South East Asia are consistent with the model in this chapter. First, the crises were large and very sudden. Countries went from a good to a bad equilibrium in a matter of weeks. Second, once beliefs coordinated in the bad equilibrium, even though different countries tried different policies in response, which changed the fundamentals and would have shifted the best responses favorably, this was not enough to get back to the good equilibrium.

A final example reinforces this account. At the same time as South East Asia was in turmoil in the first half of 1998, Russia was going through a deep recession. On August 18, 1998, the government unexpectedly decided to impose capital controls and default on its government debt. Between July 1998 and January 1999, the ruble depreciated by 262%. In figure 5.3 the interest rate on government debt reached almost 50%, reflecting the loss of value of these bonds. This created large losses in U.S.-based hedge funds and mutual funds, which, facing margin calls, sold investments all over the world. On the other side of the world, Brazil saw large capital outflows, a depreciation of its exchange rate, and a dramatic spike in its interest rates, even if the trade linkages to Russia were insignificant and the two economies were not similar in economic fundamentals. Similar events took place in Argentina, Chile, Colombia, Mexico, and Venezuela.[4]

Notes

1. On the modeling of fire sales and liquidity, see Shleifer and Vishny (2011) and Brunnermeier and Pedersen (2009).

2. Why don't the banks issue fresh equity capital? New equity holders may be wary of investing in the bank if they worry that there are hidden losses, or that the adverse feedback loops are about to magnify the shocks. The existing equity holders oppose having their share of the bank fall and thus realize a loss as well as give away some of their control over the bank. Usually, rather than getting in new equity, banks instead see their equity depleted during crisis times as existing equity holders try to channel funds out of the bank.

3. On the ΔCoVaR estimates, see Adrian and Brunnermeier (2016).

4. To read amore about these crises, see Radelet and Sachs (1998), Corsetti, Pesenti, and Roubini (1999), and Kaminsky, Reinhart, and Végh (2003).

6

Solvency and Liquidity

MOST CAPITAL flows, whether domestic or across borders, take the form of debt contracts. This is true both of the flows between banks and of foreign investment in sovereign bonds. The preference for debt comes in part because debt imposes an obligation to pay a fixed amount. This saves the lender from having to collect information about the borrower and the project's profitability. It is sufficient to evaluate whether the debtor has sufficient revenues in the present and in the future with which to repay the maturing debt.

At the same time, institutions often create a maturity mismatch when funding their projects. Even though the project can take a while to yield its payoff, the debt that funds it matures before that and has to be rolled over, often many times over. Lenders benefit from this mismatch because they can exert some discipline on borrowers, refusing to roll over the debt if they suspect the borrower is not steering the project safely and diligently. When refinancing needs arise before the final cash flow occurs, if no new funds are found, then the project has to be sold off.

This combination of debt contracts and refinancing needs creates a distinction between solvency and liquidity. An institution is solvent if the discounted net present value of future net cash flows exceeds the amount owed. Even if solvent, it can be illiquid if it cannot raise the funds to refinance the debt contracts coming due. In that case, funding liquidity is low. At the same time, it cannot sell off the project without taking on a large loss from a price discount because market liquidity is low.

Because solvency depends on future revenues, the interest rate used to discount them will determine the assessment of solvency. Any economic institution that has future revenues and some debt will be insolvent at an arbitrarily high enough interest rate. Moreover, if future cash flows are more risky, the relevant discount rate is higher since it also has to reflect a risk premium.

Liquidity problems can morph into solvency problems as the rise in interest rates and the early termination of projects can reinforce each other and spread across the financial system.

With imperfect financial markets, institutions can be solvent, but illiquid. Even if an institution's discounted future cash flow stream is positive, financial frictions can make institutions unable to roll over and keep on servicing their debt. This distinction matters because the rise in interest rates during a liquidity run makes it more likely that some institutions and projects fail, leaving behind losses to society in bankruptcy costs. Policy can potentially help, but being able to distinguish between an insolvent and an illiquid institution becomes the key diagnosis of the crisis.[1]

6.1   Debt and the Challenging Illiquidity-Insolvency Distinction

Assume that everyone is risk neutral and values the future as much as the present, so any discounting of the future is due to financial frictions. An institution comes into the market needing to refinance an amount q to keep a project going into the next period. If it survives, the project will have a random payoff z. Specifically, the payoff can take any value between 0 and 1 with equal probability, so that its expected value is $1/2$.

The institution can only issue debt contracts that may default. The contract stipulates that in exchange for q today, the creditor is entitled to a face value payment of F in the future. If the payoff turns out to be higher than the promised payment, then only F must be paid; the remainder stays with the entrepreneur as her profits. If the payoff is lower, then the most the institution can give its creditor is whatever z turns out to be.

The left panel of figure 6.1 illustrates this payoff by plotting the face value of the debt F on the vertical axis against the actual payoff of the project z on the horizontal axis. The upward-sloping line is the 45 degree line. If the promised face value payment is F_{low}, then when z is below F_{low}, the payoff of the debt is equal to the 45 degree line, as the debt-holders get paid the whole residual value of the project, which is below what was promised. If the payoff z is above F_{low}, then the payoff of the debt is equal to the horizontal line as only F_{low} is paid.

Likewise, for a higher promised debt payment F_{high}, the default probability is higher for a higher F since now, if the project's payoff z turns out to be below F_{high}, there is default. But if there is no default, the payment is of course higher.

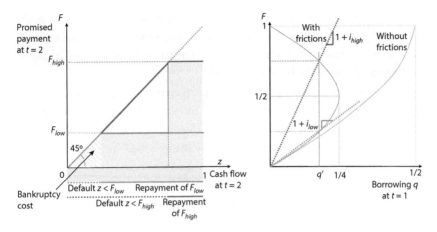

FIGURE 6.1. Solvency and liquidity with debt

The expected payoff to the lender is equal to the expected payment when the borrower defaults plus the actual promised payment when the debt is paid in full. The expected payment when there is default is equal to the expected value of z when $z < F$. The expected payment when the debt is paid in full is equal to the promised payment F times the probability that $z \geq F$. Graphically, given a uniform distribution, it is the area below the bottom horizontal line for F_{low}, or below the top horizontal line for F_{high}. Alternatively, it is the sum of the shaded rectangle and the triangle to its left.[2] For the maximum amount of promised payment, $F = 1$, the firm always defaults, and the lender is effectively an equity-holder in that she keeps the whole value of the project. The expected (net) return payoff it can promise is $1/2$, the area of the triangle for $F = 1$.

Consider now a financial friction beyond the restriction to debt contracts: the presence of bankruptcy costs. When a firm defaults, some value is lost in that some of the payoff from the project disappears. Insolvency is a costly process; when a creditor seizes an asset, it cannot generate as much cash flow out of it as the entrepreneur would have done with her ideas and skills. We will consider an extreme and simple version of this friction: triggering default always leads to the entire value of the project being lost. Lawyers, bankruptcy court fees, and disgruntled borrowers tearing down the project before it is seized combine to eat away all of the payoff. With financial frictions, therefore, if $z < F$, the lender and borrower both get nothing as the whole of z is lost. Now, the total overall payoff of the project depends on how the project gets split between the institution and the creditor.

The expected payoff of a promised debt of F is now given only by the probability it gets paid times the payment.[3] Graphically, in the left panel of figure 6.1, this is the area of the shaded rectangles. The triangles drop out of the payoff as they are eaten by the bankruptcy cost.

Compare now the two debt contracts portrayed in the figure that have different promised repayments, F_{low} and F_{high}. They have the same expected payoff for the lenders, represented by the shaded area below F_{low} and by the shaded area for F_{high}, which is partially hidden by the previous one. This is because the contract with a higher promised face value of the debt is less likely to pay it back. At the extremes, a debt contract that has a face value above 1 and one that has a face value of 0 are both worthless. The former because it is never paid back as it always triggers default, and the latter because it is always paid back but gives only 0. Since the lenders are risk-neutral and have no time preference in our example, the expected payoffs represented by the shaded rectangles coincide with the amount q the borrowers can raise for rollover financing first.

The right panel of figure 6.1 then plots the amount q that the borrower can raise at first on the horizontal axis against the promised payoff on the debt on the vertical axis. In the absence of bankruptcy costs, an increase in F leads to an increase in q as depicted by the upward-sloping curve. As depicted in the left panel, a higher face value of the debt raises the expected payment of the debt given by the area consisting of the rectangle and the triangle left of it. Thus, the amount that can be borrowed increases as well. The institution is solvent as long as the amount that it needs to borrow is less than $1/2$, which is the point on the curve when $F = 1$.

With bankruptcy costs, the rectangle alone on the left panel captures the amount that can be raised at first. On the right panel, the amount borrowed that matches the expected payoff on the debt (q) is related to the amount promised (F) through a parabola with a backward-bending part. The right peak of the parabola is at the point when the promised payment is $1/2$, which, since it pays with probability $1/2$, gives an expected repayment of $1/4$. This is then the maximum amount that lenders are willing to refinance.

The institution is insolvent if it needs to borrow more than $1/4$, that is, any amount to the right of the parabola, since borrowers would get a negative return from investing in the firm, lending more than they expect to get back. Note that the slope of a ray from the origin to the parabola gives the promised gross interest rate paid by the loan, $1 + i = F/q$, as it is the promised face value divided by the loaned amount q. Obviously, the interest rate is higher the higher F is.[4]

However, even if the institution has to raise in the present fewer funds q than $1/4$, it might not be able to do so. If no single lender has q, then the face value F that each lender asks for depends on what other lenders require. There are two possible equilibrium outcomes. If others require only a low face value, say F_{low}, the amount of funds that can be raised is given by the area on the left panel, denoted by q' on the right panel (x-axis). If so, default only happens for very low realizations of the cash flow z. In other words, the bankruptcy probability is low and that is why investors are willing to lend at a low face value F_{low} (equivalently, a low promised interest rate). However, if other lenders require a high face value F_{high}, the default is more likely as it occurs for more possible realizations of z. Given the implied high default probability, a single lender would also require the high face value (or interest rate). There is a second equilibrium outcome that gives the same funding q' (the two rectangles have the same area), despite the fact that the borrower promises a much higher face value. In this case an institution that had to refinance less than $1/4$ but more than q' is solvent but illiquid.

The economy can suddenly jump from the low to the high face value (illiquidity) equilibrium. Lending has strategic complementarities: if all other lenders only lend at the high face value (interest rate), an individual lender also requires a high face value (high rate). In contrast, if all other lenders are willing to lend at the lower face value, default probability is lower and so each lender is satisfied with a lower face value. In sum, if the market believes that debt levels are sustainable and default is unlikely, it charges a small interest rate, and a higher debt level is sustainable. If instead the market believes that the probability of default is high, then the interest rate rises, this lowers the sustainable debt limit, and default is indeed more likely.

However, the borrower (and society) is worse off with high interest rates in a liquidity crisis. The default probability is higher, so it is more likely that the large social costs of default materialize. The triangles to the left of the shaded rectangles in the left panel of the figure measure the expected social costs of default due to the financial friction, which are the resources that are lost through the bankruptcy procedure. Alternatively, the horizontal distance between the upward-sloping curve and the parabola in the right panel measures these expected losses. With a higher promised payment F_{high}, the costs are higher than with F_{low}.

The institution can try to avoid being caught in this illiquid equilibrium by reducing the amount q it needs to borrow. One way is to hold some assets with high market liquidity that can be sold easily and with little price drop. Cash is a particularly liquid asset. If the equilibrium switches, the institution can use these assets to borrow less. Another way is to avoid the maturity mismatch between the project's completion and the debt in the first place. If the institution is able to have debt that only needs to be repaid when the payoff z is realized, it avoids the rolling over that can lead to a crisis.

This analysis applies whether the borrowing institution is a firm, a bank, or a country, as long as it issues debt. If the borrowing entity is the government, future cash flows z are fiscal surpluses, which are particularly difficult to predict since they are affected by politics. There is a limit to the fiscal surpluses that a country can earn, both because there is a maximum to tax revenues, and because the government is committed to providing a minimum amount of services and paying pensions and public wages, but these commitments can change over time. This added political uncertainty also makes sovereign debt prone to liquidity and solvency crises.

Institutions like the IMF can provide foreign policy support to countries in trouble. Consider a negative shock to fundamentals so that the payoff z of the project, understood as the future fiscal surpluses, is now lower (the rectangle below the horizontal axis). The peak of the parabola is therefore now lower and interest rates rise. The country may have been close to the peak in the first place, so that even a small negative shock pushed it to insolvency, justifying the extreme increase in interest rates. Or perhaps it was not, but the shock triggered a change in lenders' beliefs from the liquid part of the parabola to the illiquid part. In this case, the rise in interest rates was due to a liquidity crisis. As it is hard to estimate the peak of the parabola, so is the distinction between insolvency and illiquidity.

If the country is insolvent, then foreign help amounts to a transfer of funds. It lowers the required q that must be financed to below the peak. This solves the crisis in the debtor country but, understandably, foreign taxpayers are usually reluctant to grant these transfers of value. If instead the country is only illiquid, then a commitment to lend to it at a fixed low interest rate with a face value of the debt that is higher than F_{low} but lower than F_{high} can be enough to eliminate the crisis. With the bad equilibrium off the table, since the country would go to the IMF instead, private creditors can coordinate on the good equilibrium. No wealth is transferred. From the domestic perspective, if the country is insolvent, it is best to default right away, renegotiate debt, and move forward. If it is illiquid, then it can try to withstand market turbulence and gain time to prove that it is solvent, convincing creditors to move to the good equilibrium. Which of the two is the crucial diagnosis that policymakers must make.[5]

6.2 The Run on the German Banking System in 1931

If illiquidity problems are not addressed in time, they morph into a solvency problem. They can spread and bring the whole financial system down and even impair the real economy.

On May 11, 1931, an Austrian bank called Creditanstalt failed. On July 13, 1931, the second largest bank in Germany, the Danatbank, went bankrupt, leading to a system-wide banking crisis in Germany. Danatbank was not contractually linked to Creditanstalt. But the failure of the first stoked fears among the creditors of banks across Europe, and triggered a shift into the equilibrium where Danatbank became illiquid. Soon after, the whole German financial system had a systemic meltdown, which contributed to the Great Depression, hitting this country especially harshly and contributing to the rise of Adolf Hitler.

The meltdown took place in three phases. First, German banks refused to lend to each other in the interbank market. In the second phase, the wholesale market also dried up. Finally, retail depositors ran on their banks. At that time there was no deposit insurance. Initially, people only reshuffled demand deposits, withdrawing funds from one bank and redepositing them with other (safer) banks. Later, the run occurred on the whole system.

As banks faced increased funding liquidity problems, they sold off their liquid asset holdings. Figure 6.2 depicts the decline of assets across the banking system in the shaded areas. While banks also cut back on loans, the decline in interbank lending and liquid securities was sharper. One banks' reduction in interbank liquid asset holdings is another bank's reduction in funding liquidity, since when one bank no longer buys short-term debt from the other banks, then they must sell their short-term liquid assets and lend less to other banks. The lines in figure 6.2 depict the liability side of the consolidated banking system, showing that, initially, primarily the interbank borrowing declined, followed by a sharper decline in deposits in June 1931.

Typically, in the case of a liquidity run, the central bank steps in and acts as a lender of last resort. However, in this case the Reichsbank, the German central bank, was constrained by the Gold Standard, which mandated covering 40% of the circulating currency with gold reserves. As the run intensified, the Reichsbank lost more and more gold reserves. To avoid breaching the gold

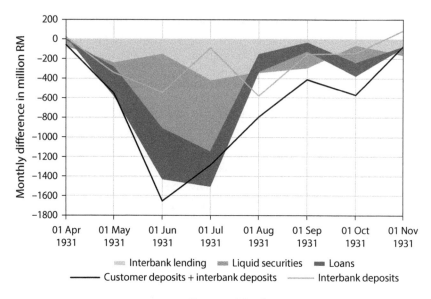

FIGURE 6.2. Germany's banks in 1931

coverage ratio, it raised the interest rate at which banks could borrow from it and tightened the collateral requirements in these loans, thus making private bank borrowing from the central bank more difficult. It did so to try to stop the outflow of gold from the country that came with the financial crisis, but this amplified the financial crash. Ultimately, it had to stop its liquidity support to the banking system entirely, rendering the Danatbank illiquid and triggering widespread panic, which was only contained by a banking holiday.

The 1931 German meltdown showed how illiquidity problems spill over across banks and countries and morph into deeper solvency problems. The German banking crisis only receded by March 1932 after the government merged the failing Danatbank with Dresdner Bank and claimed a third of the equity of Germany's largest bank, Deutsche Bank.[6]

6.3   The Greek Sovereign Debt Crisis of 2010–12 and the IMF

In October 2009, the Greek government revealed that its statistical agency had been underreporting the level of public deficit and debt for as much as a decade. In the previous two years, the public deficit had been high as a result of the global recession, but the previous estimate of a deficit of 3.7% for 2009 was replaced with a new estimate of 12.5%. On January 12, 2010, the European

Commission released a harsh report stating that it had little faith even in the new numbers and pointing to problems in the financing of social security, hospitals, and public enterprises. The perceived capacity of the Greek government to pay its debts was now lower and, at the same time, all the publicity likely triggered a revision in the beliefs of the creditors.

The interest rate on 10-year Greek sovereign debt was 4.5% at the end of September 2009. By the end of January 2010, it was 7.0%. By July it was in the double digits, and 18 months later the interest rate was 26%. Was this the result of higher perceived insolvency of Greece, or rather the result of a liquidity crisis?

Figure 6.3 shows estimates of the market-perceived probability at each date that Greece might default at any time in the next five years. These are constructed from the insurance premia that investors were willing to pay in order to get insurance against this scenario. In May 2010, after a spike in the perception of insolvency, the IMF and the EU announced a 3-year rescue package, which included a credit of up to €110 bn at the IMF's fixed interest rate. One week later, the EU created a new institution, the European Financial Stability Facility (EFSF), with a lending capacity of €440 bn, and the ECB announced a Securities Market Program (SMP) whereby it would buy sovereign bonds. All of these institutions had faith that Greece was facing a liquidity problem. Reassuringly, Greek interest rates fell sharply, from 8.9% at the start of May to 7.8% in the middle of the month, consistent with the official programs eliminating the bad equilibrium.[7]

Perceptions of insolvency, however, stayed high. One month later, Moody's credit agency labelled Greek bonds "junk" given their high likelihood of default. In October, in the town of Deauville, the French President and the German Chancellor announced that their countries would not fully pay for Greek debts, but require private creditors to lose some of their credits. The perception of default rose, crossing 50%, and reaching 70% by June 2011. At this time, the French and German governments further insisted on "private sector involvement," starting the process of negotiating what would be the residual value of Greek bonds that creditors could claim in case of a default. Perceived default spiked again, and another credit agency (Standard & Poor's) followed by assessing the risk of insolvency as very high.

By then, the official creditors had changed their mind relative to one year before. The EU postponed a second rescue package for Greece, and the IMF admitted in its July review that the debt was not sustainable "with high probability." Insolvency was by then admitted by all, and by October 2011 the EU

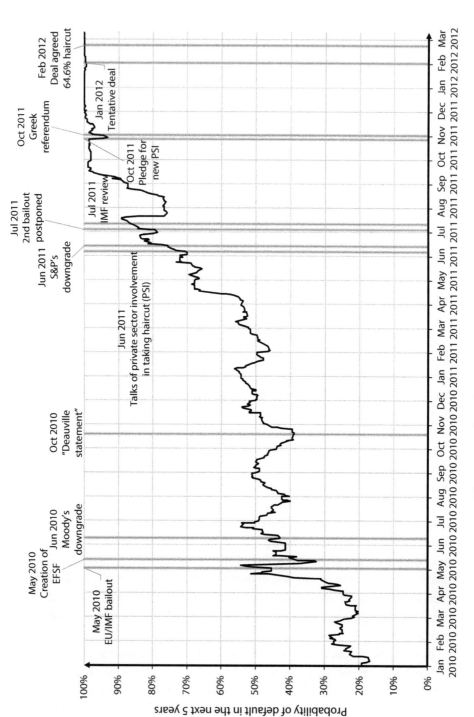

FIGURE 6.3. The perceived insolvency probability of Greek sovereign bonds

was proposing that creditors accept losing 50% of the amounts lent. After a new Prime Minister's taking over and another tentative offer in January, by February 2012, Greece indeed defaulted on its bonds. Creditors exchanged €177 bn of old Greek bonds for new bonds with a present value that was 64.6% lower.

Looking back, perhaps it should have been clearer that Greece was insolvent right at the start of 2010. Between then and the actual default two years later, there was a dramatic reversal of private capital flows, which in the previous decade had flown into Greece, and now ran for the exit. During this time, total capital inflows also fell, but much less dramatically, as public capital flew in to replace the private capital. As the official credit gets slowly paid over the years, the future will tell how much value the EU countries transferred to Greece.

At the same time, similar capital flows and spikes in interest rates happened in Italy, Portugal, and Spain. None of them defaulted on their debt and, after only a few years of public capital inflows, they were able to return to relatively lower interest rates. This suggests that they were perhaps illiquid, and that the problems in Greece may have triggered the shift in beliefs to the bad equilibrium which the EU/IMF programs helped to eliminate. Yet, at the start of 2010, in comparison to Greece, Portugal had twice as high net external foreign debt, Italy's GDP per capita had grown 45% less in the previous ten years, and Spain's banks were in worse shape. The more general lesson is that in real time, distinguishing insolvency and illiquidity is an almost impossible task.[8]

Notes

1. For more on how short-term debt can act as a disciplining device over borrowers, see Calomiris and Kahn (1991) and Diamond and Rajan (2001).

2. Mathematically, the expected payment with default is $(1 - F)F$, the product of the probability and the payment. The expected payment when the debt is paid in full is its probability F times the expected value $F/2$. Their sum is $F - F^2/2$, which gives the expected payoff of the lender.

3. Mathematically, this is: $(1 - F)F$.

4. Mathematically, if i is the interest rate on the debt, then $q(1 + i)$ is equal to the expected payoff of the debt, which is $F - F^2/2$ without financial frictions and $F - F^2$ with financial frictions.

5. More on financial frictions and solvency versus liquidity is in Brunnermeier, Eisenbach, and Sannikov (2013).

6. The figure and background material is drawn from Blickle, Brunnermeier, and Luck (2019).

7. The CDS figure uses data on 5-year Greek bond CDS spreads, and calculates the implied probability of default over the duration of the contract assuming that default arrives as a Poisson event, and that the recovery rate is 35.4%, the value it turned out to be according to Cruces and Trebesch (2013).

8. For more on the Greek crisis, see Gourinchas, Philippon, and Vayanos (2016) and Chodorow-Reich, Karabarbounis, and Kekre (2019).

7

The Nexus between the Private and Public Sectors

BANKS OUTSIDE of the United States typically hold a significant amount of national debt. There are several reasons for this.

First, financial regulation forces banks to hold a fraction of their assets in safe securities, and the rules of financial regulation treat the debt held by a government of its sovereign as riskless, ignoring a possible default. In other words, banks are not required to set any equity cushion aside for holding government debt. When default risk on this debt is high, the public debt pays a high interest rate, and this becomes an attractive investment relative to alternatives that require holding equity capital.

Second, banks hold government bonds knowing that they are accepted as favorable collateral by central banks. By holding government bonds as assets, banks make sure they will have access to central bank liquidity if necessary. They especially do so during fiscal crises, borrowing from the central bank using risky government bonds as collateral.

Third, public debt markets in many countries are organized so that banks first buy government bonds from the government during the public issuance and then resell them over time to other private investors. Banks are primary dealers of government bonds, an activity which gives them profits, but which requires them to often warehouse government bonds for some period of time, until they find a buyer for the bonds.

Fourth, because the regulator of banks is the government who must find buyers for its risky debt, it often uses "moral suasion" to pressure banks to buy its bonds beyond what their risk-return characteristics would recommend. This may well be desirable: because a banking crisis often has deep costs on the overall economy, by making banks hold many government bonds, the government is able to commit not to default. This eliminates the high interest-rate illiquidity equilibria discussed in chapter 6.

At the same time, banks often count on both explicit and implicit guarantees from the government. Explicitly because governments insure some bank deposits in order to reduce the incentives to run on banks. Implicitly because, if a bank is large enough, its failure spills over to many sectors that rely on banks to handle payments and provide short-term credit as part of their normal operations. To avoid these large economic costs, governments often choose to bail out banks in trouble, even if no official guarantee existed beforehand.[1]

7.1   The Diabolic/Doom Loop

The effect of this concentration of national bonds held by national banks and of government guarantees to banks is a diabolic (or doom) loop. Imagine that, because of a liquidity crisis, investors raise their perceived default risk on government bonds. An increase in the interest rate of new bonds implies that older bonds held by banks are now worth less. This loss is significant and gets amplified through spirals and adverse feedback loops, thus leading to cuts in lending. First, with the drop in the bank's equity, the likelihood that the government guarantees will be triggered rises. This possible extra spending also worsens the fiscal balance, lowering the value of government bonds further and weakening banks' balance sheets. Second, banks lower their lending to the rest of the economy, which reduces economic activity, which lowers tax revenues and raises government spending. The government's finances therefore deteriorate.

The loops across balance sheets also arise within the private sector. Consider, for illustration, the behavior of home builders and households. When banks cut credit and raise interest rates on their loans, home builders have to fire sell their housing stock when its market liquidity is low. Worse, they have to abandon half-finished buildings, which destroys wealth, as the earlier investments are irreversible. Since households cannot obtain mortgages so easily anymore and possibly face higher interest rates on their mortgages, any personal shock forces them to also fire sell their houses. As a result, construction activity falls and the real estate sector enters a crisis. But, as construction companies suffer heavy losses and homeowners become delinquent in their mortgage payments, the value of securitized mortgage products also falls, which further hurts the banks, feeding back into further losses in the financial system. Economic activity as a whole can be dragged down to the equilibrium

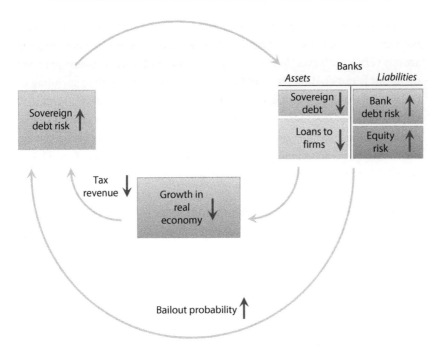

FIGURE 7.1. Diabolic loop between sovereign risk and financial risk

with low or depressed activity. This lowers the government's tax revenue, which, in turn, makes a sovereign default more likely. The loops across balance sheets contribute to the amplification of shocks across different markets that are connected with each other in the overall economy. Systemic crises spread to the real economy and back through a general-equilibrium propagation of the initial shock. Figure 7.1 illustrates the diabolic loop.[2]

7.2   European Banks and Their Sovereigns in 2007–10

European banks were especially prone to hold national sovereign bonds. Each country's sovereign bonds were treated as fully safe by regulators throughout the crisis, even in cases where the country's fiscal situation was near insolvency. The ECB's policy, in the absence of a euro-wide safe bond, was to accept sovereign bonds of every country in exchange for reserves. The public debt markets of each individual sovereign are often not very liquid, especially for smaller countries, increasing the reliance on banks as primary dealers. Finally, given the history of frequent defaults, some of the countries in the periphery put great value in the commitment provided by banks holding public debt.

At the same time, the guarantees given by the government to banks were both extensive but also more fragile. In almost every European country there are few very large banks. As a result, the commitment of their sovereign to bail them out is not credible. It would take a large amount of public spending to bail out even a single bank, and there is little room in the public budget for it.

The diabolic loop was particularly acute in the European crisis, as illustrated by figure 7.2. The top panel plots the default probability of banks and the sovereign for Ireland between the start of 2007 and the end of 2010.[3] The large Irish banks suffered losses in 2007 and 2008, partly as a result of losses in the American subprime market.[4] In September 2008, the Irish minister of finance issued a broad government guarantee to the banks, thus enhancing the diabolic loop. As the figure shows, the risk of banks and sovereigns became tightly linked, even more so when the banks failed and the government had to bail them out. The figure also shows the evolution of bank and sovereign risk for Greece during the same period. As Greece had trouble borrowing from abroad early in the crisis, Greek banks started holding a very large amount of Greek bonds on their balance sheets. The diabolic loop was very strong, so when sovereign risk rose, bank risk rose, and vice versa.

The bottom panel of figure 7.2 presents this association more systematically by plotting the monthly averages of these proxies for default of banks against those of sovereigns. Also included is data for Italy in the more recent 2014–17 period, when risk of default was not as high. The correlation continues to be large. The diabolic loop is an unsolved problem of the euro area. The positive association is clear, and it is even higher for Italy in 2014–17 than it was for Greece and Ireland before.

There have been different attempts to break the diabolic loop. For instance, in the spring of 2013, the head of the Eurogroup of finance ministers defended in an interview the view that, from then on, banks that failed should default on their senior bonds rather than being bailed out by governments, as had just happened in Cyprus. Within a few hours, bank stocks across Europe dropped but the sovereign government bond yields stabilized, as the diabolic loop was reduced. Later on, political pressure led to the recall of this statement.[5]

7.3   Argentina's 2001–02 Crisis

Throughout the 1990s, Argentina experienced high growth and low inflation, having its exchange rate tightly pegged to the U.S. dollar since 1991 through a currency board (an arrangement whereby the local currency issued is backed

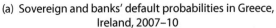

(a) Sovereign and banks' default probabilities in Greece, Ireland, 2007–10

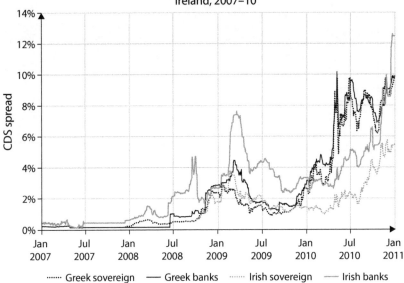

······ Greek sovereign   —— Greek banks   ······ Irish sovereign   —— Irish banks

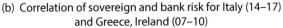

(b) Correlation of sovereign and bank risk for Italy (14–17) and Greece, Ireland (07–10)

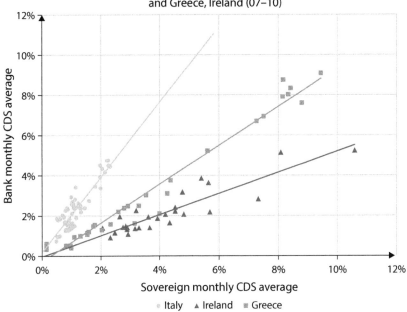

· Italy   ▲ Ireland   ■ Greece

FIGURE 7.2. The European sovereign-bank nexus

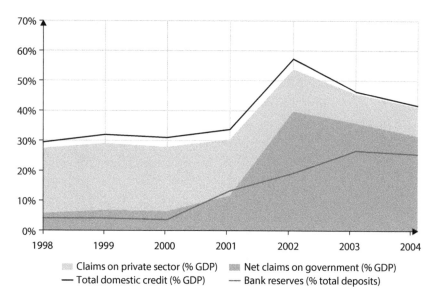

FIGURE 7.3. Bank credit to private sector and government, and deposits
at the central bank in Argentina

by foreign currency held in reserves). At the same time, some pressure was
mounting. In spite of moderate public deficits, there was persistent off-budget
fiscal spending in payments to suppliers and growing social security expenses.
The 1998 crisis that started in Brazil and that spread to its neighbors, combined
with a fall in soybean prices, created a recession in Argentina in 1999–2000.[6]

In March 2001, the minister of finance resigned after being unable to imple-
ment measures to contain the fiscal deficit, and Congress refused to cut
government salaries and pension costs. Further attempts to reign in spending in the summer were ineffective as provinces started issuing their own
bonds. Between October 2000 and July 2001, ratings agencies downgraded
Argentina's sovereign bonds five times.

Throughout 2001, the government found itself increasingly unable to roll
over its debt owed to foreigners. Aside from turning to the IMF for loans,
it forced domestic banks to buy these bonds. As figure 7.3 shows, both the
share of credit going to the government, as well as the deposits of the banks
at the central bank increased significantly during 2001. On the December 23,
2001, the government unexpectedly defaulted on its debt. Banks suffered large
losses. At the same time, bank deposits that were denominated in dollars were
converted into the less valuable domestic currency. The one-for-one currency

peg between the peso and the U.S. dollar was given up. This triggered several runs on the banks, and a suspension of withdrawals for periods of time. A serious banking crisis resulted.

Excluded from borrowing abroad because of its default, the government and the central bank borrowed heavily from the banks, crowding out lending to private firms. As the figure shows, in 2002, credit to the private sector shrank significantly, even as capital controls kept deposits domestically. The banking crisis and public finances crisis fed off each other, resulting in a deep recession. Output fell by 11% in 2002.

Forcing banks to hold government liabilities is a common form of financial repression when government bonds are hard to sell and their interest rates are high. The more direct way of doing it is to raise the requirement that banks hold zero-interest paying deposits at the central banks (sometimes called required reserves). Recently, more common have been macroprudential regulations that require banks to hold safe and liquid assets as a share of their liabilities. Government bonds are counted as the only safe and liquid asset, even when they are far from being so. A slightly more subtle approach is to force banks to roll over government liabilities for long periods of time, even as runaway inflation ensures that their real value is debased.[7]

Notes

1. In most economies, there are many tight links between banks and governments that cover the different chapters so far. Often, the public sector has a large weight in some sectors, namely education, health, and construction through public works, so government guarantees and other subsidies encourage banks to allocate capital to these sectors as discussed in chapter 3. Banks lend directly to governments, especially at the regional level, and to public companies, which are then particularly illiquid, with the consequences discussed in chapter 4. In smaller countries, even if, outside of crises, government bonds are easy to sell, during a sovereign debt crisis they can become quite illiquid, and be subject to fire sales triggering the strategic complementarities discussed in chapter 5. As we discussed in chapter 6, the distinction between solvency and liquidity is relevant for governments and companies alike. Since banks lend to both, solvency and liquidity spill over to banks as well.

2. On the diabolic loop, see Brunnermeier et al. (2016). Brunnermeier et al. (2011) first called this phenomenon the diabolic loop; Obstfeld (2013) preferred calling it the doom loop; Farhi and Tirole (2018) dubbed it the deadly embrace; Acharya, Drechsler, and Schnabl (2014), the bank-state nexus; and policy speeches in Europe often refer to it as the adverse feedback loop. We use the original term, but they are all equivalent.

3. Credit default swap (CDS) spreads measure the insurance premia charged in markets to guard against default. In the figure, we average the CDS for the three largest banks in the country.

4. These were amplified through the funding spirals we discussed in chapter 5.

5. For European evidence, see Acharya, Drechsler, and Schnabl (2014), Altavilla, Pagano, and Simonelli (2017) and Ongena, Popov, and Van Horen (2019).

6. Discussed in chapter 5.

7. For more on the Argentinian episode, see Sturzenegger and Zettelmeyer (2006). On the diabolic loop across the world, see Gennaioli, Martin, and Rossi (2018).

8

The Flight to Safety

A PARADOXICAL feature of financial crises is that, even as interest rates across many sectors and regions all spike up, the interest rates in some other asset classes and regions become unusually low. These price movements reflect a flight of capital to safety. As investors shift their portfolios away from assets they deem to be risky and toward those that they deem to be safe, the price of the latter rises. This shift from a risk-on to a risk-off mode can amplify financial crises because these price changes reinforce the perception of relative risk across the assets.

Within countries, this shift naturally occurs from equities to government bonds as the former are perceived as riskier in their payoffs than the latter. Across regions, this happens as capital flies from emerging markets to advanced economies, as the latter are perceived to be safer. Capital flows across borders come with trade flows in opposite directions, and, more generally, with macroeconomic implications.

The fact that investors flee from risky assets and rush into safe assets raises an important question: what is a safe asset in the first place, and what are its important characteristics? A safe asset is a precautionary savings instrument. It can be used as a safe store of value that can be sold at a relatively stable price after an adverse shock.[1]

8.1   Safe Assets

To better understand the concept of a safe asset, consider two people, Alice and Bob. They are averse to risk, and face some individual risk in the form of some unexpected expenses, say to repair a car or to pay for health care. Assume that their risks are perfectly negatively correlated. When Alice faces a negative shock, Bob faces a positive one, and vice versa. Ideally, Alice and Bob should insure each other, but suppose this is not possible due to financial frictions.

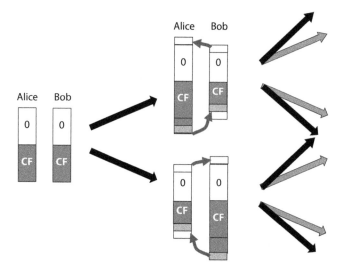

FIGURE 8.1. Trading a safe asset between Alice and Bob

They can, however, both hold an asset. Its market is depicted by the white rectangles in figure 8.1. For simplicity, say that this asset does not ever pay any cash flows; hence the zero in the rectangle. Seemingly it has no fundamental value. The other asset, depicted by the shaded rectangle, has a positive cash flow (CF). However, if Alice faces a negative shock and Bob a positive one, their shaded boxes shrink and expand, respectively, and Alice can sell the asset to Bob in return for a payment. This is represented by the right downward-pointing black arrow. In the case when Bob faces a negative shock and Alice a positive one, the opposite trade occurs. This case is shown by the right upward-pointing black arrow in figure 8.1. So, the person with a loss receives a positive cash flow asset in exchange for a zero cash flow asset.

Even though Alice and Bob cannot directly insure each other, they can do so indirectly by holding a (zero cash flow) safe asset and re-trading after the shocks are realized. This makes the asset useful and valuable. It may not give a cash flow, but it gives a service flow in the form of self-insurance via re-trading. This highlights the first characteristic of a safe asset. Like a good friend, it is there and valuable when Alice or Bob needs it.

On top of this, the safe asset might appreciate if both Alice and Bob suddenly face more risk. Graphically, figure 8.1 reflects this with the black arrows to the right that depict larger random changes relative to the gray arrows. Suppose we are going into a recession and, as is typical, people's aversion to risk is rising during these hard times. The extra indirect insurance service that a safe asset provides is then even more valuable to Alice and Bob. They want to self-insure more and increase their precautionary safe asset holdings. Hence, the value of the safe asset rises in times of crisis. In other words, the safe asset is a good friend to everybody in risky times, not only when a particular idiosyncratic risk materializes.

The second characteristic of a safe asset is its easy tradability. This is ideally achieved if the cash flow of the safe asset is the same across a wide variety of possible future scenarios. The holder does not need to investigate what is more or less likely to happen in the future and does not need to worry that other traders know more about the cash flows than he does, letting them take advantage of him when trading.

Finally, the third characteristic is that the safe asset status is largely self-fulfilling: an asset is safe if it is perceived by most to be safe. This last property is at heart a tautology. In times of crisis, risk perceptions rise. Investors then flee from risky assets and rush into safe assets, which reinforces their safety.

Typically, government bonds take on this role within a country. Global reserve assets, like the U.S. Treasury Bond, the German Bund, and the Japanese Government Bond, take on this role for international finance. Not surprisingly, countries are eager to issue safe assets since their low required return makes them a cheap source of funding. In times of crisis, safe assets gain in value, which makes it easier for governments, which can issue a safe asset to finance various stimulus measures in order to stabilize their economies in recessions. This, in turn, makes the country's government bond more resilient against the macro shock. This mechanism adds another self-fulfilling element to the safe-asset status.

Of course, a country's debt may lose its safe-asset status if, for example, a debt restructuring is seen as becoming increasingly likely. In that case, capital may flow to a foreign safe asset, which further amplifies the stress a country's economy is under. As investors withdraw their risky funding, firms feel funding pressure, slowing down investment projects. Consequently, the overall economic growth rate slows down further, making a default of the domestic government even more likely.

8.2   Borrowing Costs in the Euro Area: The 2010–12 Crisis

In the euro area, there is no euro-wide government bond to serve as a safe haven. The perceptions of risk apply to regions as opposed to asset classes, so

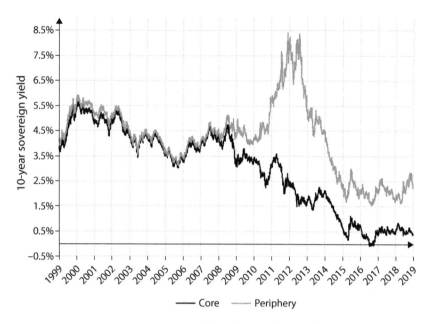

FIGURE 8.2. 10-year sovereign yields in the periphery and core of Europe

the flight-to-safety capital flows become cross-country capital flows. Figure 8.2 plots the sovereign yields between the start of 1999 and the end of 2018 for the euro area core countries (Germany and France) and its periphery countries (Greece, Ireland, Italy, Portugal, and Spain).[2] Before the crisis, the yield on sovereign bonds of all these countries was approximately the same, suggesting that all could be safe assets.

Between the start of 2010 and the end of 2012, the two series diverged sharply. Even seemingly innocuous statements from policymakers during this time would throw markets into a frenzy with sharp run-ups and rapid falls in national interest rates in the periphery. At the same time, yields in the core steadily fell to historically low levels. These sharp increases in the spread between the two rates came with large capital flows from the periphery to the core and deep recessions in the periphery.

Why were German bonds perceived to be safe while Greek bonds were not? The gap in yields can arise in response to three sources of risk, as investors require a higher compensation ex ante to bear this risk. The first is that the exchange rate of the periphery currency can depreciate relative to the core, so that when converted to the same units, the return is lower than the stated interest rate. The introduction of the euro in 1999 had eliminated the perception of exchange rate risk between the two regions since they now shared a single currency. However, in 2010, it re-emerged in the form of "re-denomination risk." The risk was that debt in euros would be re-denominated into new national currencies worth less than the euro; effectively, a default. As an example, financial contracts went from putting the probability that Greece leaves the euro at below 1% in 2007 to above 50% in 2010. In July 2012, as the spread peaked, the president of the ECB Mario Draghi affirmed that ". . . the ECB is ready to do whatever it takes to preserve the euro. And believe me, it will be enough." Perceptions of this risk fell sharply and so did interest rates.

The second source of risk is the possible loss of the safe asset status. Government bonds from vulnerable euro countries became less desirable precautionary savings instruments. If others do not find it useful to save and self-insure with these bonds, then each individual finds it less useful too. In other words, since these bonds' service flow declined, investors asked for higher cash flows in the form of higher interest rates. In contrast, government debt issued by the core countries became more attractive as safe assets and hence their yield declined, leading to capital flows from the periphery to the core of the euro area.[3]

Third, losing the safe asset status forces peripheral countries to pay higher interest on their bonds. This increases their interest burden, making their government debt level less sustainable, and a default more likely. This increase in default risk increases the interest rate further. The Maastricht Treaty imposed a bailout clause that made it formally illegal for other European institutions to bail out countries with debt problems. The reasoning behind this constraint was that making default risk explicit would eliminate inflation risk arising due to fiscal problems, as the ECB would not be forced ex post to debase the real value of the debt by inflation. Moreover, making default risk explicit was a way to activate market discipline, and have countries that fail to follow disciplinary budget rules face a higher interest rate. Additionally, the increase in default risk for peripheral government bonds makes them information-sensitive: their payoffs are not kept constant across various circumstances. Hence, well-informed investors can take advantage of uninformed ones. They withdraw and markets freeze. In addition, a bad illiquidity equilibrium outcome can arise when governments have to roll over large amounts of debt, as we discussed in chapter 6.

An alternative solution is to attack the root of the problem: the asymmetry between the bonds and their underlying fiscal situations across different regions. A common bond solves the problem from the start because it imposes

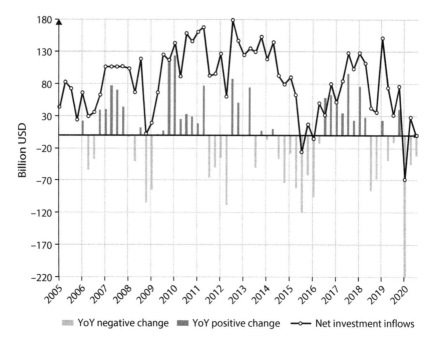

FIGURE 8.3. Net capital flows to emerging economies

a single equilibrium with no cross-region flights to safety. Importantly, such a bond can be designed without one country having to guarantee another country's debt.[4]

8.3   The Pandemic Flight to Safety of 2020

Figure 8.3 shows the quarterly net capital flows going to the aggregate of 21 emerging markets, for the sum of direct investment or portfolio investments in the balance of payments. Sometimes these rise (bars above the horizontal axis), and sometimes they fall (bars below the horizontal axis), but for almost every single quarter between 2005 and 2019, these flows were positive, with a brief and small exception in 2015 (a period that became known as the "taper tantrum"). In 2020, the Covid-19 pandemic took over the world. Between January and February, countries in Asia adopted drastic measures to contain the spread of the virus. In March, most countries in Europe as well as many cities in the United States entered a lockdown. Economic activity in the second quarter of 2020 fell by record levels in most countries in the world, and there was great uncertainty on how bad the health and economic damage would be.

Such a large and unprecedented shock triggered a large flight to safety. In the second quarter of 2020, a striking $70 bn of investments flew from emerging markets into the advanced economies, a decline of $220 bn relative to second quarter of 2019. Advanced economies during that quarter were harder hit by the pandemic than emerging economies. Yet, the perception that their financial markets were safer attracted capital. This may seem perverse, but it was consistent with the economic forces we discussed in this chapter: an even larger negative shock to the core countries can be more than offset by an increase in uncertainty across the world, and trigger the flight to safety from the periphery to the core.

At the same time, the Federal Reserve fiercely protected the safety of the U.S. Treasuries market, by buying U.S. government bonds from those who wanted to sell them, lending against them for those who needed liquidity, and supporting dealers in the market where they are traded. A combination of good policy and good luck reverted this shift in the following two quarters. Whilst the capital that left the emerging markets did not go straight back, the outflow stopped right away. At least for 2020 and early 2021, a crisis in emerging markets was averted.

Notes

1. On modeling safe assets, their characteristics, and the flight-to-safety phenomenon, see Brunnermeier, Merkel, and Sannikov (2022) and Calvo (1998).

2. We calculate these aggregate variables by a weighted average of the country variables, with weights given by the GDP of each country, averaged over the period. The yields refer to the 10-year government bond yields.

3. On the capital flows in the euro area see Lane (2012).

4. How to design such a bond is crucial so that it does not create more problems than the ones it solves. A bond where all regions are jointly liable for the payments, like a Eurobond, so that if one does not pay the others must cover the shortfall, creates great moral hazard. An alternative that removes the joint and several liability, and so does not create these distortions, is the issuance of sovereign bond-backed securities (SBBS or ESBies). For details see Brunnermeier et al. (2011) for the euro area and Brunnermeier and Huang (2019) for global emerging market economies.

PART III

Policies and Recoveries

9

Exchange Rate Policies and the Speed of Recoveries

FOR A small open economy, the speed of recovery from a recession—its resilience—partly depends on the relative price of its domestic goods and services in terms of their foreign counterparts—the real exchange rate. If the real exchange rate falls (so it depreciates), then the country's exports become cheaper, and its imports more expensive. Domestic expenditure switches from foreign to domestically produced goods, so the differences between the two—the trade balance—moves toward a surplus. This boosts production at home and allows the economy to recover.

The strength of this expenditure switching channel depends on how quickly and how much the real exchange rate depreciates. Domestic goods can become cheaper either because the domestic prices fall relative to the foreign prices, or if the nominal exchange rate—how many units of foreign currency one can get in exchange for one unit of the domestic currency—depreciates. In most economies, goods and services' prices are sluggish to adjust, but nominal exchange rates are financial prices that can move quickly. Therefore, most of the adjustment of the real exchange rate happens through changes in the nominal exchange rate. A common policy recommendation that is followed by most advanced economies is to have their nominal exchange rate freely float. This way, when a recession comes, the real exchange rate can swiftly depreciate, triggering a quick bounce back of economic activity. Flexible exchange rates can make economies more resilient to shocks.

Recessions that are driven by financial crises change this logic and prescription. On the one hand, the initial force for the exchange rate to depreciate is stronger than in other recessions, since it partly results from capital fleeing from the country. As it does, investors sell the domestic currency, which causes the nominal exchange rate to fall, and so the real exchange rate depreciates. On the other hand, there are new channels through which this depreciation of the exchange rate affects the economy.

A prominent one is that emerging economies often borrow through banks in foreign currency, creating a mismatch on their balance sheets, since assets and revenues are in domestic currency, while liabilities and the expenses in paying the debt are in foreign currency. When the exchange rate depreciates, the value of these debts in domestic currency rises as does the cost of servicing the debt. Investment can therefore fall significantly and stay depressed even as consumption and output start recovering. If this negative impact on the liabilities of banks and firms is strong enough, they can become zombies, saddled with debt, and only slowly rebuilding their net worth by retaining earnings. This can further slow down the recovery and resilience. In extreme cases, the depreciation's negative effect on investment may more than offset its positive effect on the trade balance, and output falls. In this case, the exchange rate depreciation amplifies the downturn, instead of attenuating it. The policy advice is now different: capital controls or exchange rate interventions that prevent, or slow down, the depreciation may have some merits.[1]

9.1   A Model of Exchange Rates and Recovery

In equilibrium, investment must equal the sum of domestic and foreign savings. Domestic savings are the difference between output (Y) and the sum of private and public spending. From abroad, foreigners save in the domestic economy when they send more of their goods in exchange for fewer domestically produced goods, so the domestic economy is running a trade deficit.

When income rises, for fixed spending, savings rise. However, with higher income, private spending also rises, so that the increase in savings is smaller than the increase in income. Moreover, higher income comes with higher purchases of goods from abroad, which raises the trade deficit, and so increases foreigners' savings. Depending on whether the effect of higher income on private spending domestically or abroad is higher or lower, savings may rise more or less than one-to-one with income. Either way, savings rise, as shown by the solid upward-sloping line in figure 9.1, for the case where the slope of the relation is smaller than 1.

Also in the figure is an investment function. With frictionless financial markets, investment depends only on comparing the marginal returns from those investments against the marginal cost of funds for the firms, but not on the

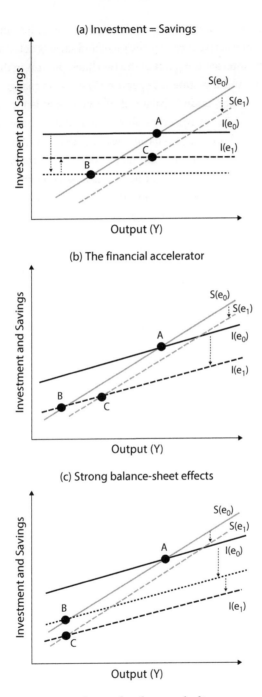

FIGURE 9.1. Internal and external adjustment

level of output. Therefore, the function is a horizontal line in panel (a) of figure 9.1. The internal balance of investment and savings determines the level of output at the intersection point of the two lines, point A in the figure.

Both savings and investment depend on the real exchange rate (e). In a long-run equilibrium, trade is balanced, the economy is increasing neither its borrowing nor its savings from abroad, and the real exchange rate e is approximately 1. This is the purchasing power parity condition dictating that domestic and foreign goods must ultimately sell for the same real price. At any date though, the economy may not be in this long-run equilibrium, and the exchange rate may be different from 1, affecting both savings and investment.

Starting with savings, if the exchange rate appreciates (e rises), then domestic exports become more expensive for foreigners to buy, while imports are cheaper for domestic agents to buy. The direct impact is for the trade balance to worsen. At the same time there is an indirect effect in the opposite direction, since less is being paid per unit imported, which would improve the trade balance. The Marshall-Lerner condition states that the direct effect exceeds the indirect effect if the elasticities of exports and imports to the exchange rate are large enough. If so, which we assume to be the case, then a depreciation makes the savings curve shift down, as foreign savings in the domestic economy have fallen.

Turning to investment, some of the capital flows that support investment come from abroad, so they depend on the willingness of foreigners to lend to the domestic economy. If the exchange rate is temporarily appreciated relative to its long-run value, then it must be expected to depreciate. In that case, foreigners expect a loss in units of foreign currency from their lending in domestic currency to domestic firms, so they require a higher return to do so. This lowers investment, so that higher e shifts the investment function down.

All that remains to understand is what determines the exchange rate itself. The value of the exchange rate at a point in time is determined by an external balance: for the economy to have a trade deficit, foreigners must be saving in the domestic economy, so capital is flowing in from abroad. The trade deficit is higher with an appreciated currency. Capital flows are lower due to the expected depreciation. Where the two are equal determines the equilibrium real exchange rate.

With this simple model of what determines output and the exchange rate behind it, we can analyze the impact of a financial crisis. Starting from the equilibrium at point A in panel (a) of figure 9.1, imagine that foreigners, perhaps driven by a fear of insolvency or by a flight to safety, become less willing to lend to the domestic economy. Internally, firms are able to borrow less, so the investment curve shifts down. For a fixed exchange rate, the economy moves to point B. Output falls, as the economy enters a recession. Eventually, faster or slower, the real exchange rate adjusts, either through a depreciation of the currency, or through a fall in domestic prices relative to foreign prices. This must happen to restore external balance. This depreciation shifts savings to the right and investment upward, so the economy moves to point C, a swift recovery made possible by the exchange rate adjustment. Policy would like to speed this adjustment of the real exchange rate by floating the currency. This way, the nominal exchange rate can do most of the work, as opposed to inflation, which tends to be more sluggish.

Panels (b) and (c) of figure 9.1 incorporate financial market imperfections, which modify the benevolent view of sharp recoveries aided by large depreciations. Investment depends not only on the costs of borrowing, but also on sales. When a firm can generate more revenue, it is able to borrow more against it, because lenders become reassured that the firm is viable and that, in case of distress, it will be able to keep on servicing the debt. Moreover, firms with higher cash flows can use them as a cheaper source of funds to invest. These cash flow effects translate into an upward-sloping investment relation, as portrayed in panel (b). The crisis that results from the initial shock is now amplified, as point B is now further to the left than before. The recession leads to less investment by firms, which in turn reduces real activity further. This is called the financial accelerator effect, and it makes the economy more volatile. The depreciation would still act as a stabilizing force.

A second financial channel changes the effects of the depreciation. As the value of domestic assets is lower when expressed in foreign currency, the collateral that domestic firms can offer to foreign lenders is now worth less. Moreover, in many economies, domestic banks borrow abroad in foreign currency (usually the U.S. dollar). The depreciation then raises the value of the liabilities of banks in units of domestic currency, but not the value of their assets, which consist of loans to firms and other financial assets that are denominated in domestic currency. This mismatch between the currencies of assets and liabilities has been called the original sin, as it causes large falls in net worth and possibly bank failures when there is a sharp depreciation.

Firms and banks with less net worth following a depreciation have less skin in the game to reassure their borrowers that they are committed to repaying. All combined, the investment function now has a force making it shift down when e falls. Moreover, firms that borrow in foreign currency will also want to price their goods in that currency, to match the currency of their interest expenses and sales revenues. If so, the depreciation no longer makes the domestic goods cheaper. This also reduces the stimulative effects of a fall in e on foreign trade, by making the rightward shift of the savings curve smaller.

Panel (b) of figure 9.1 shows the case where the balance-sheet effect just offsets the impact of cheaper borrowing and so the depreciation leaves the investment curve unchanged. In this case, the economy recovers to point C, with significantly lower output than in panel (a). Importantly, the recovery is driven by consumption and the trade surplus, while investment and capital flows remain depressed. This has been called a Phoenix recovery, as the economy emerges from the ashes of a recession caused by an investment crunch, even as investment itself barely recovers.

If the depreciation harms the domestic banks' and firms' balance sheets by more, then the investment curve shifts down as a result of the depreciation. This is portrayed in panel (c), where point C is now only slightly to the right of B, so the economy barely recovers. Whether the economy is characterized by panels (b) or (c) depends on the state of domestic balance sheets, the extent of the original sin, the size of the shock itself, and the level of financial development of the economy, as they all affect the impact of the depreciation on financial conditions. The effect of the depreciation on the recovery can then be state-dependent, as opposed to unambiguously supportive. The depreciation can even deepen the recession if the boost to exports is more than offset by the cut in lending to firms and banks with impaired balance sheets. Capital controls or exchange-rate intervention policies that prevent the sudden depreciation, allowing net worths to recover, can prevent the recession from becoming a depression.

This can take time because, cut off from outside funding, firms can only recover their net worth by retaining earnings. Moreover, the initial sharp recession may lead to bank failures, and with them a loss of knowledge on the creditworthiness of borrowers, which takes time to rebuild. Even if the initial shock reverts, or other policies boost the economy, the investment curve can stay depressed to the left for many years, only slowly shifting to the right. Financial crises come with slow recoveries because of the scars that they leave on credit.[2]

9.2   The Mexican Tequila Crisis of 1994–95

Starting in 1988, the Mexican government started an ambitious program of financial liberalization, economic reforms, and stabilization of inflation by pegging the peso to the U.S. dollar. The program was a success, judging by the

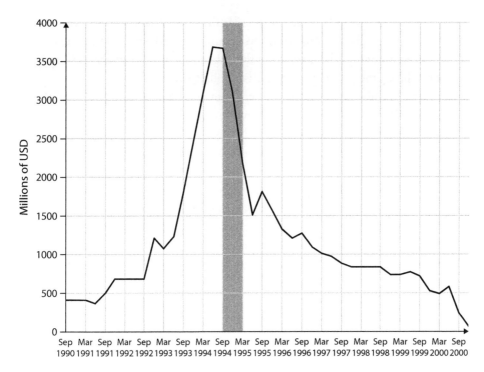

FIGURE 9.2. Outstanding Mexican debt issued in U.S. dollars

rapid increase in output and consumption, large capital inflows, the expansion in credit, and inflation remaining below two digits for several years. At the same time, and unlike in previous stabilization programs in Mexican history, the overall public sector balance was kept in a (slight) surplus, and the Mexican central bank accumulated a large stock of U.S. dollars to defend its peg. Against these solid fundamentals, there were concerns that the real exchange rate was overvalued, as the external deficit was large and growing, while the peg prevented the nominal exchange rate from depreciating.

During this time, the Mexican government had also started selling Tesobonos: dollar-denominated public debt. In 1994, two shocks hit the economy. First, the Federal Reserve raised U.S. interest rates, putting strain on the Mexican central bank to follow suit in order to keep the peg. Second, political disturbances in Mexico associated with the presidential election (including an assassination) came with increasing difficulties in rolling over the public debt. The government started rapidly converting short- and long-term peso-denominated bonds into Tesobonos, which were easier to sell. Tesobonos rose from 4% of privately held public debt to 75% within one year. Figure 9.2

shows the corresponding sharp increase in the share of debt that was denominated in U.S. dollars held by foreigners: the original sin became extreme in the Mexican economy. The maturity of the public debt also became increasingly short during the year, requiring constant rolling over.

On December 20, 1994, the Mexican central bank announced a 15% devaluation. This managed devaluation was expected to correct the perceived overvaluation of the peso in an orderly way. Instead, it failed within one day. The devaluation raised the peso value of the Tesobonos, making the needed rollovers even harder. Because the central bank's dollar reserves were only a third of the amount of public debt coming due, it could no longer pay it off while keeping the peg to the U.S. dollar. The economy entered a sharp recession, and further devaluations further raised the peso value of the debt. The country entered a spiral that, only three months later, led the peso to devalue by almost 100%, and economic activity to sharply fall. This crisis spread to Argentina and Brazil, until a loan from the U.S. government to Mexico stopped the spiral.[3]

9.3   The Lasting Stagnation from the 2008 Global Financial Crisis

Investment can stay stagnated for many years as a result of the financial accelerator and cash-flow effects. This is the case even when the trigger of these is a change in the exchange rate. Macro-financial crashes have effects that persist, as banks and firms slowly improve their balance sheets.

In September 2008, the large U.S.-based financial institution Lehman Brothers went out of business, leaving behind a large web of debts to other financial intermediaries. The uncertain spread of these losses across different institutions and markets froze financial transactions and depleted the capital of many banks, leading to a fall in credit and sharp reductions in financial wealth. With these came a decline in economic activity. For instance, the U.S. unemployment rate rose to 10%, and by 2010, U.S. real GDP was 10% below the pre-crisis trend. Many advanced economies likewise went through twin crises, with declines in both economic and financial activity. In many other economies though, banks were less active in international finance markets or had lower leverage to start with, so there was never a significant financial crisis, even if the recession touched all through the fall of global trade.

Figure 9.3 adds up the GDP in dollars across 197 countries in the world, split between those that went through a financial crisis in 2008 (22 of them) and

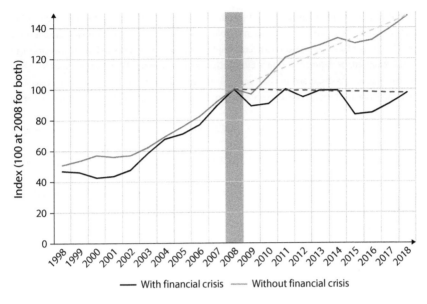

FIGURE 9.3. The lasting effects of the 2008 global crisis

those that did not, indexing the total output of each group to be at the same level in 2008. Right before the crisis, the group that later suffered a crisis had actually gone through a better decade, and its GDP had grown by 16% more than the other group's. Both groups suffered a recession, with a fall in output between 2008 and 2009. The drop in output was deeper for the countries that had a financial crisis vis-a-vis the others.

The recession was also much longer for those countries, and only ten years later had global output reached the same level as it was pre-crisis for this group. The main drag on the recovery was investment, which stayed low, as the net worth of banks and firms took a long time to return to previous levels. The group without a crisis, in contrast, was 47% richer in 2018 than it had been in 2008. The figure suggests that having a financial crisis may even have a permanent effect on trend growth.[4]

Notes

1. The expected depreciation or appreciation of the currency can lead to large anticipated losses or gains from investing abroad. Therefore, the changes in beliefs discussed in chapter 2, applied to exchange rates, are behind speculative attacks on a country's currency. On the other hand, when the exchange rate changes, so does the relative price between the goods and services

that the country trades abroad, and those that it does not, contributing to the misallocation between these two sectors discussed in chapter 3. A major difficulty in assessing the solvency and liquidity of a sovereign, discussed in chapter 6, is that low returns to foreign investors can result from either default or from a devaluation of the currency. When capital flies to safety across borders, as discussed in chapter 8, this triggers adjustments in the exchange rate. The exchange rate is a key macroeconomic price equilibrating markets, and it is a key financial price creating risk and returns.

2. The model in this section builds on Céspedes, Chang, and Velasco (2003) and Calvo, Izquierdo, and Talvi (2006).

3. Calvo and Mendoza (1996) and Mishkin (1999) provide more details on the Mexican crisis.

4. On slow recoveries after financial crisis, see Cerra and Saxena (2008) and Fernald et al. (2017).

10

The New Conventional
Monetary Policy

MANY CENTRAL banks have a dual mandate, aiming to keep inflation close to a target (often 2%) while reducing the amplitude of fluctuations in unemployment. When an economy enters a garden-variety recession, with no significant financial component, the standard response is for monetary policy to lower nominal interest rates. Insofar as inflation expectations are sticky, this lowers real interest rates, providing incentives for firms to invest more, as financing is cheaper, and for households to spend more and save less, because the return on savings is lower. This increase in spending raises aggregate demand, which raises output if prices do not fully rise in response, a phenomenon known as nominal rigidities. Thus, output is stabilized.

In the past, central banks traditionally lowered interest rates by either lowering their desired target for an interbank rate at which banks lend to each other overnight with little risk (in the case of the Fed, the Federal funds rate), or by lowering the rate at which the central bank lends a limited amount to these banks over a short period of time (in the case of the ECB, the MRO for one week). Both of these cuts in rates were achieved by increasing the amount of reserves: the deposits that banks hold at the central bank. Reserves are nothing but entries in a spreadsheet at the central bank stating how much each bank has deposited, but because the unit of these entries defines the unit of account in the economy, they are the way in which payments are settled between any two banks or between any two economic agents that use banks. Since lending in the interbank market was an imperfect substitute for reserves for banks, if reserves paid no interest, the interbank rate would give the opportunity cost of reserves. When there were more reserves, the interbank rate fell.

Since financial crises come with deep recessions, from the perspective of the dual mandate, the response of monetary policy might appear to be the same as in any other recession: cut interest rates. But there are differences in the policy tools that can be used and in their effects during a financial crisis. These are sometimes called unconventional policies, but since 2010 they have become the norm across almost all advanced-economy central banks.[1]

10.1   Reserve Satiation and Quantitative Easing

In a financial crisis, central banks are often called to be lenders of last resort to banks, replacing the missing funding, or to governments, buying their bonds to prevent their price from falling sharply.[2] This involves the central bank using its power to create reserves and give them to banks, either by buying government bonds or by accepting these bonds as collateral in loans. This reduces the opportunity cost of reserves, that is, the gap between the nominal interbank rate i and the rate paid on reserves i^v.

While this could be done by keeping the rate on reserves at 0, the large increase in their supply to provide to the banking sector or the government would imply that $i = 0$. The central bank would then lose its power to independently affect the interest rate and steer inflation and real activity. A superior alternative is to instead pay non-zero interest on reserves. As long as $i^v = i$, the opportunity cost of reserves is still driven to zero, but the central bank can now choose whatever level of i^v it wants. The effective policy tool is now the interest rate on reserves that is controlled by the central bank, not the interbank rate that it may target. With this policy, the demand for reserves by banks is satiated, which offsets the private funding crisis. The top panel of figure 10.1 illustrates the choice of the interest rate paid on reserves and the way in which this choice can lead to reserve satiation.

The change in policy tool, from the supply of reserves to the interest on reserves, and in equilibrium, from scarce to abundant reserves, arose during the financial crisis of 2008–10. However, economists have long argued that it is desirable at all times. Famously, Milton Friedman noted that since the central bank can just create reserves at no social cost by changing the entries on its spreadsheet, the private opportunity cost of reserves should be zero. Reserve satiation is sometimes called the Friedman rule, and it is particularly desirable when the demand for reserves is heightened during a financial crisis.

A second form of unconventional policy concerns the maturity of the interest rates that the central bank focuses its policy on. The interest on reserves

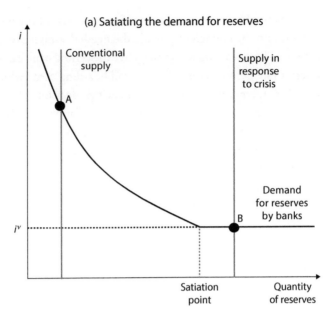

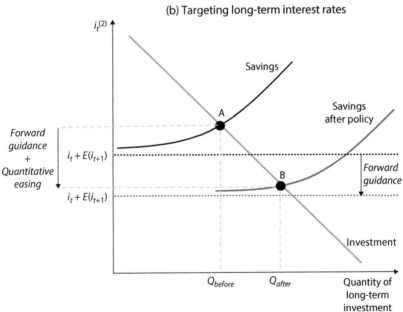

FIGURE 10.1. Unconventional monetary policy

is an overnight rate. During a deep financial crisis, bringing it down all the way may not be enough to provide the needed stimulus to inflation and real activity. There is a limit to how negative the central bank can set the overnight interest rate before people start instead hoarding cash (which pays no interest). Yet, for many investment and savings decisions, the relevant cost of financing or return on savings that affects inflation and real activity is likely not the overnight rate but rates that apply to months or years. The central bank would like to lower these longer-maturity interest rates in order to maximize the amount of stimulus it provides.

To understand how it can do so, consider a simple case where at date t, aside from the 1-period rate i_t, there is also a "long-term" interest rate at which firms and households can borrow or save for two periods: $i_t^{(2)}$. The smaller $i_t^{(2)}$, the lower the opportunity funding cost of two-period investments, and so the larger the investment in two-period projects. The bottom panel of figure 10.1 represents this as a downward-sloping line.

From the perspective of the saver, she can either invest for two periods, or roll over two successive one-period investments. However, next period's one-period interest rate is not known today, so the best the saver can do is form an expectation of it, call it $\mathbb{E}[i_{t+1}]$. If all the risk from this rollover strategy can be diversified away in financial markets, the demand for two-period savings would be a horizontal line at $i_t + \mathbb{E}[i_{t+1}]$, as portrayed in figure 10.1 by the dotted line. However, with imperfect financial markets, investors may require an extra premium, call it tp_t for term premium, to compensate for the different risk and funding needs that the two strategies may have. In the figure, this is represented by the upward-sloping savings line, under the assumption that the term premium increases if the private investors have to hold larger amounts of these risky and hard-to-sell bonds. At the equilibrium at point A: $i_t^{(2)} = i_t + \mathbb{E}[i_{t+1}] + tp_t$ holds.

A central bank that wants to lower $i_t^{(2)}$, and has already driven down the short-term interest rate i_t to the lowest possible level, can follow two unconventional strategies. The first one, called forward guidance, consists of making announcements of what future policy interest rates will be, and taking on whatever commitments are available to deliver these rates. This lowers the $\mathbb{E}[i_{t+1}]$ perceived by investors. In the graph, it shifts the demand curve vertically down. The second strategy, called quantitative easing, consists of buying government bonds of longer maturities in exchange for crediting the reserve accounts of the banks selling them. Increasing the demand for bonds at those maturities raises their price and lowers the compensation for risk that investors demand on them, thus lowering tp_t. This shifts the demand curve horizontally to the right. Combined, these two strategies lead to a new equilibrium at point B, where $i_t^{(2)}$ is lower and investment is higher.

The combination of reserve satiation and quantitative easing implies that the balance sheets of many central banks today look quite different from what they were at the turn of the century. Reserve satiation requires the balance sheet to grow, since reserves are liabilities of the central bank, while quantitative easing requires it to develop a maturity mismatch between the overnight reserves on the liabilities side and the long-term bonds on the asset side. One side effect of this is that changes in $i_t^{(2)} - i_t$ now affect the net income flow earned or lost by the central bank. Before, with a small balance sheet and no interest paid on reserves, the net income was steady and small. Now, the central bank generates or loses significant resources in the conduct of its monetary policy, so its interaction with the fiscal authorities, and the extent to which it is has their support in conducting these unconventional policies, becomes more relevant, putting strains on the independence of the central bank.

10.2   The Bank of Japan's Innovations since 1998

In the decade after its 1980s financial crisis, the Japanese economy had not just low growth, but also a mild and prolonged deflation.[3] Inflation expectations were low, and almost every year, actual inflation was well below the target of 2%. After 40 successive years of having a balance sheet at a relatively constant size, near 10% of GDP, the Bank of Japan changed track after 1995. Figure 10.2 plots the size and composition of the Bank of Japan's balance sheet.

Between July 1996 and March 1999, the Bank of Japan issued reserves, raising its liabilities, and lent them out to banks, raising the "other assets" category in the balance sheet. The loans were needed because in 1997, partly as a consequence of large losses in their investment in South East Asia, many Japanese banks were under stress.[4] The loans provided resources to the banks, who needed them to reassure depositors and other short-term funders. The supply of reserves increased, satisfying the large increase in the demand for safe liquid assets in the economy. The Bank of Japan satiated the demand for reserves, and this allowed it in the next stage to separate these financial needs from the use of the deposit rate as the main instrument for inflation policy. In 1999 and 2000, the Bank of Japan focused on inflation and used forward guidance. With the deposit rate at 0.15% in February 1999, policymakers announced the future path of the deposit rate, and the overnight interest rate in the interbank

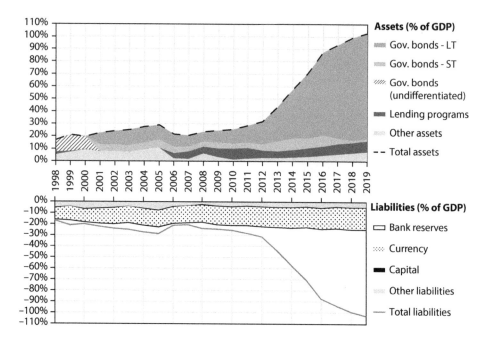

FIGURE 10.2. The balance sheet of the Bank of Japan

market stayed below 0.05% throughout 1999 and 2000. Reserves barely increased.

Starting in March 2001, and lasting until March 2006, the Bank of Japan implemented (in fact, invented) quantitative easing to try to get inflation to rise. It started steadily issuing reserves and purchasing long-term government bonds, committing to keep on doing so until the prices of goods and services would rise. The large extent of these purchases is visible in the increase in the size of the balance sheet in figure 10.2. September 2010 brought two changes. First, the pace at which reserves were issued increased. Second, the Bank of Japan tried to affect not just the term premium discussed in the previous section, but also other premia reflecting the difference between short-term bonds and other assets. For instance, the Bank of Japan also started buying corporate bonds and shares in the stock market, even if, as the figure shows, the amounts bought were never all that large.

Between 2013 and 2016, the Bank of Japan greatly increased the pace at which it expanded the balance sheet, naming these policies qualitative and quantitative easing, to reflect both the expansion in the size of the balance sheet and the purchase of different types of assets. Finally, in September 2016,

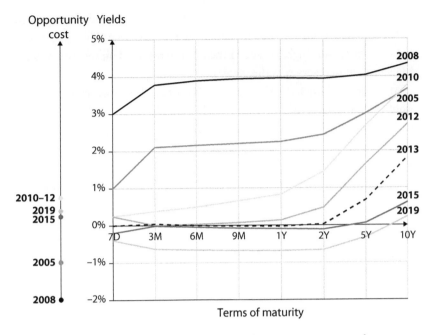

FIGURE 10.3. The euro area yield curve and the opportunity cost of reserves

the Bank of Japan announced a policy of yield curve control, where its purchases of long-term government bonds were aggressive to the point of aiming for a target for the 10-year rate. In terms of figure 10.1, the central bank started now shifting the demand curve in a fine-tuned way to target $i_t^{(2)}$ directly. After the 2008 financial crisis, most advanced-economy central banks followed in the footsteps of the Bank of Japan, first satiating the market for reserves, then introducing quantitative easing, and finally expanding the set of assets beyond just government bonds.[5]

10.3   The Euro Area Yield Curve during Crisis

A yield curve plots the sequence of interest rates $i_t^{(m)}$ for different maturities m scaled so that they are all in annual units. Figure 10.3 plots the euro yield curve at different stages in the life of the ECB.[6] The figure also plots the gap between the rate at which the ECB lends to banks at 28 days, the MRO rate (on the marginal refinancing operations, as they are called), and the interest it pays on overnight reserves, the deposit rate, using dots in the vertical line to the left. This provides a rough measure of the opportunity costs of reserves, or of how far the European banking system has been from reserve satiation.

At the start of 2005, the yield curve had its "normal" upward-sloping shape as the European economy was expanding at a regular pace. The opportunity cost of reserves was high, reflecting the low interest paid on reserves and the small amount of reserves in the system.

At the start of 2008, the U.S. financial crisis had already generated funding problems for European banks. The ECB responded to the rightward shift of banks' demand for reserves by expanding its balance sheet, and by lowering the opportunity cost of reserves through an increase in the deposit rate from 1% to 3%. At the same time, it did little to its normal interest rate policy, so the entire yield curve just shifted up, with little change in slope. Between then and the start of 2010, the euro area entered a recession. The ECB's first reaction was to provide stimulus through conventional tools, by cutting short-term rates, so the yield curve steepened.

From the start of 2010 onward, the euro crisis spilled over from the financial sector to the sovereign debt markets. The ECB not only went to the limits of conventional policy, cutting the MRO rate all the way down to 0.25%, but it also made clear that interest rates were likely to remain low into the future. While the interpretation of the legal mandate of the ECB at the time was that it could not acquire government bonds directly, it instead announced a lending program, LTRO (long-term refinancing operations), whereby banks could buy the government bonds, and give them to the ECB for a long period of time in exchange for a loan of reserves. Thus, while neither forward guidance nor quantitative easing were officially adopted, implicit versions of them were being used. As a result, by the start of 2012, the yield curve had moved down in an almost parallel shift relative to 2010's.

The ECB embraced unconventional policy in full force from then onwards. In 2012, the ECB announced, but never applied, its outright monetary transactions (OMT) program through which it could have acquired sovereign bonds from specific euro area countries in financial difficulties. The satiation of the demand for reserves went to the limit, where, by November 2013, the MRO-deposit rate gap was only 0.25%. And forward guidance was explicitly pursued from July 2013 through official statements at policy meetings that the ECB would keep interest rates low for an extended period of time. From January 2015 onward, the ECB implemented a large scale asset purchase program, its quantitative easing, and bought assets from across the whole euro area. As a result, between 2012 and 2015 the yield curve greatly flattened, and it stayed flat until 2019.

The other side of the movements in the yield curve was the change in the ECB's balance sheet. Its size grew through the satiation of reserves from 1.2 trillion at the start of 2007 to 2.8 trillion by the end of 2015, and 4.5 trillion by the end of 2017. The share of securities held outright (instead of collateralized lending programs) went from 10% at the start of 2007 to 43% by the end of 2015 and 60% by the end of 2017. In turn, within its lending programs, the share of longer-term operations went from 27% at the start of 2007 to 84% at the end of 2015 and 100% by the end of 2017. In undertaking these policies, the ECB took on a significant risk to its fiscal independence. Unlike other central banks that can count on commitments from the fiscal authorities to provide backing in case the central bank's equity becomes very negative, the ECB lacks clear fiscal support due to the fragmented nature of European fiscal policy.[7]

Notes

1. The role of reserve satiation in monetary policy is discussed in Reis (2016).

2. The central bank and its lending ability already appeared in several previous chapters as a remedy to some of the problems. In the discussion of banks in chapter 4, central banks can provide deposit insurance because they are able to lend unlimited amounts to banks. Some modern banks though are not covered by deposit insurance, making them particularly fragile, but even then ex post central banks will often intervene through lending programs. In chapter 5, when there are multiple equilibria, being large players in financial markets, central banks can sometimes coordinate beliefs in good equilibria. As we discussed in the Irish case, lending to banks to replace the lost wholesale funding can stop the crisis. In chapter 6, we discussed the role of the IMF in being an international lender of last resort; domestically, this role is performed by the domestic central banks. The central bank also plays a role in the diabolic loop since, as discussed in chapter 7, raising requirements that banks hold a fraction of their deposits at the central bank is a common form of financial repression. In chapter 8, the ECB played an important role first in eliminating exchange-rate risk between European regions as the euro was adopted, and then in fighting fears of re-denomination risk during the crisis, which was greatly done by buying the government bonds of periphery countries. Finally, pegging the exchange rate, as discussed in chapter 9, involves in practice controlling the supply of central bank liabilities.

3. Discussed in chapter 2.

4. This was already discussed in chapter 5.

5. Dell'Ariccia, Rabanal, and Sandri (2018) and Bernanke (2020) discuss the different stages of Japanese monetary policy.

6. Because there are no euro-wide safe bonds, as we discussed in chapter 8, this yield curve is constructed by the ECB by averaging between the interest rates of the sovereign bonds of different regions in the euro area, subject to the requisite that they are rated AAA and so are considered almost free of default risk.

7. For a description of the policies of the ECB, see Hartmann and Smets (2018).

11

Fiscal Policy and the Real
Interest Rates

THE GREAT Depression is, to this day, the queen of financial crises, as it led to the largest macroeconomic recession felt in many countries in the past century. Because fiscal policy played an important role in ending the Depression, its experience led to an understanding that public deficits should rise during recessions, which has guided macroeconomic policy ever since. There are two different bodies of arguments for why it should be so.

One of them, that often goes under the wide umbrella of neoclassical, is based on the principle that most taxes and transfer programs distort behavior, and having those distortions vary over time compounds them. When economic activity falls in a recession, keeping tax rates and the generosity of social programs unchanged implies that fiscal revenues fall and spending rises, resulting in a public deficit. Raising taxes or cutting subsidies in a recession would discourage work, production, and investment at a time when they are already depressed. Public deficits should be countercyclical, moving in the opposite direction of output.

Another argument, often labelled Keynesian, sees recessions as times when private savings are too high, above what would be socially desirable. The other side of the coin is that private spending, and so production, are too low. If the government increases spending, or cuts tax revenues, it decreases public savings and brings the economy closer to the desired point. At the same time, extra government spending raises public demand for goods, and the lower tax revenues raise private spending for goods, both leading to more output being produced.

Neither of these arguments depends on whether the recession comes with a financial crisis. If it does though, there are new forces that interact with these mechanisms. They provide further arguments for having the public deficit rise during a recession.

11.1   Savings and Investment, Revisited

The global economy is closed (we do not trade with other planets, yet), so all investment must come from someone's savings, either private or public.[1] In making their savings choices, private agents care about their real consequences and their real returns. The real interest rate r is the key relative price considered when choosing to save. The expected real return of investing in a government nominal bond, which delivers a promised payment denominated in units of currency, is equal to the nominal interest rate i minus expected inflation π^e, capturing the loss in value of the currency relative to real goods. Therefore, to a first approximation, the forces of arbitrage dictate that $r = i - \pi^e$, so that real investments and nominal bonds gives the same expected return.

When the real interest rate is higher, households will want to delay consumption and save more to take advantage of the higher returns. Therefore, the supply of savings will slope upward, as in figure 11.1. Turning to investment, as the real interest rate rises, there are fewer investment projects that have a marginal return making them worthwhile. Therefore the demand for investment slopes downward. Where the two intersect at point A determines the global equilibrium real interest rate, r^*.

An application of the neoclassical argument is to see recessions as times when productivity falls, so the demand curve shifts left. Less is invested, so for a fixed tax rate on investment, tax revenues fall. Raising the tax rate would further shift the demand curve to the left, lowering the return on investment, and deepening the recession. An application of the Keynesian view is that people become pessimistic and change their savings, moving the economy away from r^*. By having public dissavings (deficits), or public savings (surpluses), fiscal policy can shift this total savings curve back to its initial position.

This setup points to three forces that can result from a financial crisis and that lead to a decline in r^*. First, one of the main drivers of savings is households' desire to put resources aside during their working years in order to sustain a standard of living during retirement. Those savings are partly channeled to safe assets, which are produced by the dissavings of other agents in the economy, for instance, the retired households. These savings and dissavings net out to give the total savings line in the figure, which goes to finance investment.

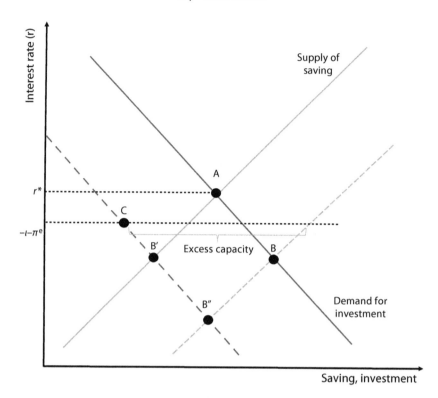

FIGURE 11.1. Investment and savings

Now, after a crisis, financial markets become less able to produce these safe assets. Households looking to dissave and households looking to save do not have the vehicles to do so, and as a result the latter turn to investing in real projects, raising the stock of capital, and planning to sell it in the future when they want to dissave. This means the savings curve shifts to the right, as shown in the figure, and so r^* falls as the economy moves to point B, along the investment curve, and so with many low-productivity investments being made. It may even be the case that r^* is so low that the economy is dynamically inefficient: every household could be made better off by consuming more instead of saving at such low returns, as long as all other households would do the same, increasing real interest rates. Public deficits after financial crises create a safe asset: government bonds. This government dissaving shifts the total supply of savings back to the left, raises r^*, and can move the economy back near point A.

A second driver of household savings is a buffer against future bad income shocks. Fearing the future loss of a job, or a disease that requires costly treatment, people save to be able to pay for unexpected expenses and to sustain their standard of living. A deep financial crisis comes with an increase in the unemployment rate, and in the risk of job loss for many workers. Deep recessions are also times when, even conditional on keeping one's job, income risk rises, as some have their hours or overtime cut and others do not. Realizing uncertainty is higher, people raise their precautionary savings. The savings curve shifts to the right again, and the economy ends up at B, with a lower r^*. There is even a multiplier effect, as less spending deepens the recession and raises risk, spurring additional savings.

There is one effective public policy against this multiplier effect of precautionary savings on recessions. All advanced economies have a safety net that provides social insurance: those who lose their jobs can collect unemployment benefits, and those whose income falls are charged lower income tax rates. If the misfortune is extreme, there is poverty relief and catastrophic health insurance. All of these lower the post-tax, post-transfers income risk faced by households. In a recession, they reduce the increase in precautionary savings, and so prevent the supply of savings from shifting to the right as much in the first place, hence stabilizing r^*. At the same time, as more people qualify for transfers and fewer pay taxes, this leads to budget deficits. Since the social insurance depends on individual characteristics, the deficits arise automatically, without any need for policy changes in response to the crisis. Because of this, they are called the automatic stabilizers.

Third, and turning to investment, the return on most individual projects has some idiosyncratic risks. Because part of those risks depends on features of the project that only the entrepreneur knows about, and because she can affect those returns through her efforts in a way that no one can accurately measure, the availability of private markets to insure against these risks is limited. Moreover, the human capital of the entrepreneur is tied to the project, since without her the project's assets would not be as productive. Therefore, the entrepreneur's own financial resources must be used in the business so that she has skin in the game to employ her human capital.

In a financial crisis, this idiosyncratic investment risk rises through multiple channels. Private insurance markets retreat, so less risk can be diversified. Banks cut lending so entrepreneurs must use more of their resources to keep projects going, thus bearing more of the risk. As financial firms fail, their expertise at sorting through projects and excluding the riskier ones is lost. Often, policymakers choose to tighten financial regulations, making financial firms want to bear less risk, which is left in the hands of the entrepreneurs. All combined, this increase in idiosyncratic risk shifts the demand for investment to the left. As the economy moves to the point B' in the figure, this has a similar effect as the rightward shifts of supply: it lowers r^*. Public deficits directly shift the supply of savings to the left, raising r^* back up. Moreover, they generate government bonds, which provide a safe haven for entrepreneurs to hold in their portfolios together with their risky projects. This increases their willingness to undertake those projects, offsetting the initial decline in investment.

Another important financial consideration arises in this market during deep crises. Through all the mechanisms highlighted so far, the supply curve may shift sufficiently to the right, and the demand curve sufficiently to the left, that the new intersection may be at a significantly negative real interest rate. Taking as fixed expected inflation (because firms' prices are sticky or people's beliefs are sluggish), this new intersection may be at a value well below $-\pi^e$. Yet, this would require a significantly negative nominal interest rate. This cannot be so, because people would then just save in banknotes and coins. By design, currency pays a zero nominal interest rate, so that taking the costs of safekeeping it, its expected return is only slightly below zero. That return puts an effective lower bound on nominal interest rates in the economy; call it $-\iota$ (the reversal rate). The effective lower bound on real rates is $-\iota - \pi^e$.

If the intersection of demand and supply for savings is at a rate below the lower bound, then the economy is not at point B″ shown in figure 11.1. Rather, the economy is at point C, where the real rate is at the lower bound, and desired savings exceed investment. The other side of the coin of this excess savings is deficiency in production and consumption. The recession is deeper at C than it would have been at B″.

A budget deficit that shifts the savings curve leftward, at first has no effect on real interest rates. Therefore, a unit of higher public deficit leads directly to a one-unit increase in investment, which may then lead to higher increases in output, using the spare capacity in the economy. Outside of the effective lower bound, deficits raise interest rates, which crowds out some private investment. At the lower bound, budget deficits have higher multipliers, a measure of their impact on output. Moreover, because the increase in government spending will tend to raise inflation expectations, it will lower the effective lower bound, which by itself stimulates the economy by allowing the real interest rate to fall further.[2]

11.2   The Rise of Savings during the 2020 Pandemic

Between February and March 2020, many Western advanced economies locked down their economies in response to the Covid-19 pandemic. This caused record-breaking single-quarter falls in GDP. The recession affected economic sectors and people in disparate ways. Many people kept their jobs, adjusted to remote working, and had little fall in income. Many others found their revenues drop to zero and were suddenly unable to stay afloat. Governments responded with very large transfers to firms and households to prevent business failures and alleviate economic deprivation.

In the United States, these transfers were so large that disposable income of the private economy, which is equal to national income plus net transfers, rose by an astounding 8.0% between 2019:Q3 and 2020:Q3. In spite of national income falling, for one year the government paid out much more than it received in taxes. In the other direction, in the European Union, where the fiscal support provided by the government was smaller and the recession deeper, disposable income fell by 3.7%. The United Kingdom was in between, with disposable income rising by 2.5%.

Figure 11.2 shows savings rates in the three economic areas. In all of them, savings spiked in 2020, increasing by factors between 2 and 5, something that had not been seen for decades. There are at least two ways to make sense of this increase and to explain what will follow.

One is to argue that consumption fell during 2020 because people could not have access to many of their usual consumption goods and services. Therefore, these were "compulsory" savings. In that case, savings would fall and overshoot relative to their usual values as the pandemic ended and economy activity opened in full. Having over-saved during 2020, households would be eager to adjust their stock of savings back to a desired level, going on a large spending boom. This would push economic activity to recover swiftly from the recession. Further government deficits would be unnecessary, and fiscal policy would want to turn to paying off the public debt accumulated during 2020 instead.

Instead, perhaps the increase in savings partly or fully reflected an increase in precautionary savings. Households that were worried about their health and economic well-being, perhaps because of pessimism about the end of the pandemic, perhaps because they anticipated lay-offs and business failures, may have been saving more because their perceived individual risk was higher. In that case, the high stock of savings may have persisted into the future. One would still have seen a spending boom in 2021 and 2022, as the flow of savings adjusted, but it would not be as extreme.

Importantly for the readers of this book, understanding the macro-financial components of the 2020 recession sheds light on the trade-offs that

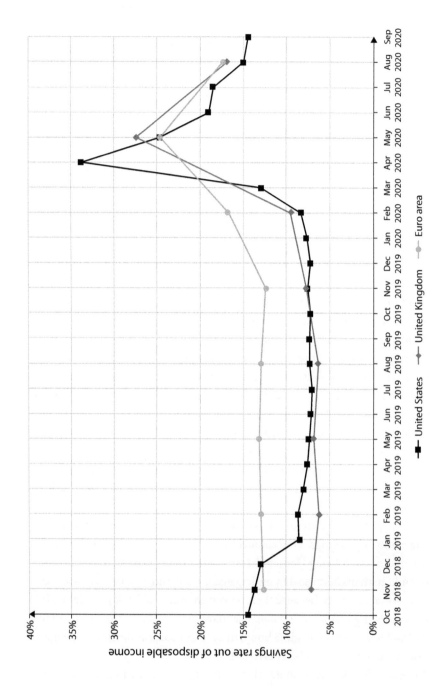

FIGURE 11.2. Savings rate out of disposable income

policymakers face, and points to what should be measured and understood to try and sort out what the dominant forces are.

11.3 The End of the U.S. Great Depression

Between 1929 and 1933, the United States went through the deepest recession in the nation's history. In October 1929, the stock market crashed, with the Dow Jones index of prices losing 25% of its value in only five days; it would take until 1954 for it to return to its previous peak. At the beginning of 1933, 52% of all farm mortgage debt was delinquent on its payments. A wave of bank failures meant that by 1933, only slightly more than half of the banks that existed in 1929 were still in operation. In the macroeconomy, industrial production fell continuously for four years—typical postwar contractions have lasted only 1 year—and the size of the decline in output was between 30% and 40%, depending on the measure used. The U.S. Great Depression is still the mother of all macro-financial crises.

From the start of the Depression and until the mid 1940s, 3-month nominal interest rates were almost zero. John Maynard Keynes famously blamed the fall in private spending and the fall in real interest rates at the outset of the Depression as the result of "animal spirits" of people wanting to save more in response to all the uncertainty, and in doing so causing income to fall even more so that in the end less was saved (the "paradox of thrift"). At the same time, between 1929 and 1933 the U.S. economy experienced deflation, with the price level falling by a cumulative 30%. While there are no direct measures of inflation expectations for the time, historians have argued that households, firms, and investors expected prices to continue falling. With negative expected inflation, the effective lower bound may well have been close to zero. All combined, the economy was, for more than a decade, captured by the situation at point C in figure 11.1.

The recovery started in 1933, coinciding with the election of Franklin D. Roosevelt (FDR). With it came an abrupt change in U.S. policy, which included a concerted effort to raise inflation expectations and let the U.S. dollar lose value relative to the gold standard. More famously, the spending programs of the New Deal came with large public deficits and government dissavings. The economy rebounded quickly in the following four years, with output growing 29% and prices 13%.

A second event, soon after, provides some support for the view that government deficits can stimulate the economy during macro-financial crises,

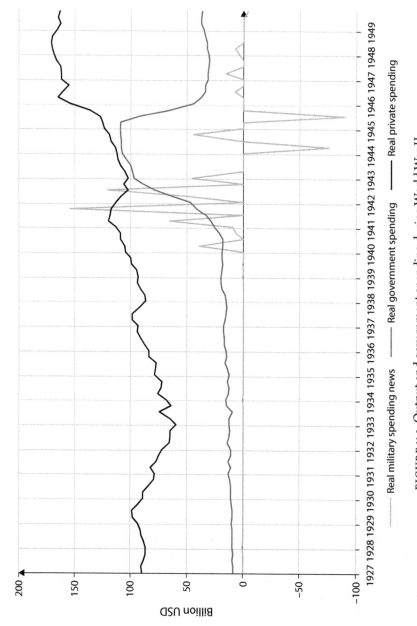

FIGURE 11.3. Output and government spending during World War II

——— Real military spending news ——— Real government spending ——— Real private spending

Billion USD

1927 1928 1929 1930 1931 1932 1933 1934 1935 1936 1937 1938 1939 1940 1941 1942 1943 1944 1945 1946 1947 1948 1949

especially at the effective lower bound. The U.S. recovery stalled between 1937 and 1938, as output per capita had just reached its pre-depression peak, leading to fears that the macro-financial crisis would permanently leave the nation poorer.[3] Yet, growth accelerated from 1940 onward, so that by the second half of the decade, output was back on its trend line. This second stage of the recovery coincided with World War II, which began in September 1939 in Europe, and which the U.S. entered in December 1940.

At the start of 1940, it seemed very likely the United States would enter the war, and military spending ramped up. Figure 11.3 shows both actual total government spending, which increased from 15% at the end of 1939 to almost 50% by 1944, and a series that captures news about planned future military spending. Unsurprisingly, the plans predate the actual spending. In the figure is also the path of output, which accelerated once spending was planned and announced. Formal econometric estimates using these data find that while the impact on output of defense spending is usually less than 1, when the economy is at the effective lower bound, it jumps to 1.5.[4]

Notes

1. The models in chapters 9 and 10 discussed how foreign savings finance domestic private investment, and how central banks can affect nominal interest rates, respectively.

2. See Rachel and Summers (2019) on the evolution of r^* and what might be behind it, Ravn and Sterk (2017) on how precautionary savings can deepen recessions, McKay and Reis (2016) on the role of the automatic stabilizers, and Eggertsson and Egiev (2020) on multipliers when interest rates are zero.

3. Chapter 9 discusses the persistent, and sometimes permanent, effects of macro-financial crises.

4. See Ramey and Zubairy (2018) and Ramey (2019) for further discussions of the evidence.

PART IV

Parting Words

12

Conclusion

ECONOMIES SOMETIMES go through macro-financial crises. These are neither solely crises in financial markets, with large changes in asset prices and trading volumes but limited impact on the macroeconomy, nor are they conventional macro crises for which the financial sector has a secondary role in transmitting shocks to fluctuations in output and employment. Rather, macro-financial crises have their source or major amplification in the financial market, they have large macroeconomic effects, and the interaction between macroeconomic policy and financial institutions occurs through multiple reinforcing channels.

This book introduced readers to ten concepts in macro-finance that are central in a crisis. In the run-up to the crisis, bubbles arise and persist as each investor is trying to anticipate what others will do. The large capital inflows that arise from chasing bubbles, financial liberalization, or optimism, come with real misallocation between and within sectors. The banks that intermediate these funds see their balance sheet change as leverage increases and funding becomes collateralized by marked-to-market securities.

After an initial shock, liquidity spirals and fire sales generate strategic complementarities that amplify the shock or create multiple equilibria leading to systemic failure in the financial market, propagating to real activity. In the heart of the crisis, the previous use of debt makes it difficult to distinguish between solvency and liquidity, which produces wide fluctuations on interest rates paid. At this time, the holding of government bonds by banks links the financial sector to government fiscal policy in a way that brings both down together. As investors flee for safety, regional imbalances in the supply of safe assets can produce costly capital flows.

In the recovery, investment stays depressed, and a depreciation of the exchange rate hurts debtors, slowing down the economy. Central banks can provide liquidity to banks and help markets distinguish between a solvency and a liquidity crisis, but to fight the recession, they must also resort to unconventional monetary policy, in the form of reserve satiation, forward guidance, and quantitative easing, all of which have an effect on different interest rates by changing the composition of the central bank balance sheet. Fiscal policy must tame the demand for safety by raising public dissavings or providing automatic stabilizers, while paying attention to the composition of spending and its associated multipliers.

Together, and related to each other, these ten concepts provide tools to understand how macro-financial crises emerge, grow, and can be attenuated.

BIBLIOGRAPHY

Acharya, Viral V., Itamar Drechsler, and Philipp Schnabl. 2014. "A Pyrrhic Victory? Bank Bailouts and Sovereign Credit Risk." *Journal of Finance,* 69(6): 2689–2739.

Admati, Anat, and Martin Hellwig. 2014. *Bankers' New Clothes.* Princeton University Press.

Adrian, Tobias, and Markus K. Brunnermeier. 2016. "CoVaR." *American Economic Review,* 106(7): 1705–1741.

Altavilla, Carlo, Marco Pagano, and Saverio Simonelli. 2017. "Bank Exposures and Sovereign Stress Transmission." *Review of Finance,* 21(6): 2103–2139.

Arellano, José Pablo. 1985. "De la Liberalizacion a la Intervencion: El Mercado de Capitales en Chile 1974–1983." *El Trimestre Económico,* 52(207(3)): 721–772.

Bernanke, Ben S. 2020. "The New Tools of Monetary Policy." *American Economic Review,* 110(4): 943–83.

Blickle, Kristian, Markus K. Brunnermeier, and Stephan Luck. 2019. "Who Can Tell Which Banks Will Fail?" Princeton manuscript.

Brunnermeier, Markus K. 2009. "Deciphering the Liquidity and Credit Crunch 2007–2008." *Journal of Economic Perspectives,* 23(1): 77–100.

Brunnermeier, Markus K., and Lasse Heje Pedersen. 2009. "Market Liquidity and Funding Liquidity." *Review of Financial Studies,* 22(6): 2201–2238.

Brunnermeier, Markus K., and Lunyang Huang. 2019. "A Global Safe Asset for and from Emerging Market Economies." In *Monetary Policy and Financial Stability: Transmission Mechanisms and Policy Implications.* Vol. 26 of *Central Banking, Analysis, and Economic Policies Book Series,* ed. Álvaro Aguirre, Markus Brunnermeier, and Diego Saravia, Chapter 5, 111–167. Central Bank of Chile.

Brunnermeier, Markus K., and Stefan Nagel. 2004. "Hedge Funds and the Technology Bubble." *The Journal of Finance,* 59: 2013–2040.

Brunnermeier, Markus K., Luis Garicano, Philip Lane, Marco Pagano, Ricardo Reis, Tanos Santos, David Thesmar, Stijn Van Nieuwerburgh, and Dimitri Vayanos. 2016. "The Sovereign-Bank Diabolic Loop and ESBies." *American Economic Review Papers and Proceedings,* 106(5): 508–512.

Brunnermeier, Markus K., Thomas Eisenbach, and Yuliy Sannikov. 2013. "Macroeconomics with Financial Frictions: A Survey." *Advances in Economics and Econometrics, Tenth World Congress of the Econometric Society.* New York: Cambridge University Press.

Brunnermeier, Markus, Luis Garicano, Philip R. Lane, Marco Pagano, Ricardo Reis, Tano Santos, David Thesmar, Stijn van Nieuwerburgh, and Dimitri Vayanos. 2011. "European Safe Bonds (ESBies)." Manuscript at www.euro-nomics.com.

Brunnermeier, Markus, Sebastian Merkel, and Yuliy Sannikov. 2022. "Debt as Safe Asset." NBER working paper 29626.

Calomiris, Charles, and Charles Kahn. 1991. "The Role of Demandable Debt in Structuring Optimal Banking Arrangements." *American Economic Review*, 81(3): 497–513.

Calvo, Guillermo A. 1998. "Capital Flows and Capital-Market Crises: The Simple Economics of Sudden Stops." *Journal of Applied Economics*, 1: 35–54.

Calvo, Guillermo A., Alejandro Izquierdo, and Ernesto Talvi. 2006. "Sudden Stops and Phoenix Miracles in Emerging Markets." *American Economic Review*, 96(2): 405–410.

Calvo, Guillermo A., and Enrique G. Mendoza. 1996. "Mexico's Balance-of-Payments Crisis: A Chronicle of a Death Foretold." *Journal of International Economics*, 41(3): 235–264.

Castillo-Martinez, Laura. 2020. "Sudden Stops, Productivity and the Exchange Rate." Duke University manuscript.

Cerra, Valerie, and Sweta Chaman Saxena. 2008. "Growth Dynamics: The Myth of Economic Recovery." *American Economic Review*, 98(1): 439–57.

Céspedes, Luis Felipe, Roberto Chang, and Andrés Velasco. 2003. "IS-LM-BP in the Pampas." *IMF Staff Papers*, 50(1): 143–156.

Chodorow-Reich, Gabriel, Loukas Karabarbounis, and Rohan Kekre. 2019. "The Macroeconomics of the Greek Depression." *CEPR Discussion Paper 13762*.

Corsetti, Giancarlo, Paolo Pesenti, and Nouriel Roubini. 1999. "What Caused the Asian Currency and Financial Crisis?" *Japan and the World Economy*, 11(3): 305–373.

Cruces, Juan J., and Christoph Trebesch. 2013. "Sovereign Defaults: The Price of Haircuts." *American Economic Journal: Macroeconomics*, 5(3): 85–117.

de la Cuadra, Sergio, and Salvador Valdés. 1990. "Myths and Facts about Instability in Financial Liberalization in Chile: 1974–1983." Instituto de Economia. Pontificia Universidad Católica de Chile. Documentos de Trabajo 128.

Dell'Ariccia, Giovanni, Pau Rabanal, and Damiano Sandri. 2018. "Unconventional Monetary Policies in the Euro Area, Japan, and the United Kingdom." *Journal of Economic Perspectives*, 32(4): 147–72.

Diamond, Douglas W., and Philip H. Dybvig. 1983. "Bank Runs, Deposit Insurance, and Liquidity." *Journal of Political Economy*, 91(3): 401–419.

Diamond, Douglas W., and Raghuram G. Rajan. 2001. "Liquidity Risk, Liquidity Creation, and Financial Fragility: A Theory of Banking." *Journal of Political Economy*, 109(2): 287–327.

Dias, Daniel A., Carlos Robalo Marques, and Christine Richmond. 2016. "Misallocation and Productivity in the Lead Up to the Eurozone Crisis." *Journal of Macroeconomics*, 49: 46–70.

Diaz-Alejandro, Carlos. 1985. "Good-bye Financial Repression, Hello Financial Crash." *Journal of Development Economics*, 19(1-2): 1–24.

Eggertsson, Gauti B., and Sergey K. Egiev. 2020. "A Unified Theory of the Great Depression and the Great Recession." Brown University manuscript.

Farhi, Emmanuel, and Jean Tirole. 2018. "Deadly Embrace: Sovereign and Financial Balance Sheets Doom Loops." *Review of Economic Studies*, 85(3): 1781–1823.

Fernald, John G., Robert E. Hall, James H. Stock, and Mark W. Watson. 2017. "The Disappointing Recovery of Output after 2009." *Brookings Papers on Economic Activity*, 1: 1–89.

Fernández-Villaverde, Jesús, Luis Garicano, and Tano Santos. 2013. "Political Credit Cycles: The Case of the Eurozone." *Journal of Economic Perspectives,* 27(3): 145–66.

Galvez, Julio, and James Tybout. 1985. "Microeconomic Adjustments in Chile during 1977–1981: The Importance of Being a Grupo." *World Development,* 13(8): 969–994.

Garber, Peter M. 2000. *Famous First Bubbles.* MIT Press.

Gennaioli, Nicola, Alberto Martin, and Stefano Rossi. 2018. "Banks, Government Bonds, and Default: What Do the Data Say?" *Journal of Monetary Economics,* 98: 98–113.

Gopinath, Gita, Şebnem Kalemli-Özcan, Loukas Karabarbounis, and Carolina Villegas-Sanchez. 2017. "Capital Allocation and Productivity in South Europe." *The Quarterly Journal of Economics,* 132(4): 1915–1967.

Gorton, Gary. 2010. *Slapped by the Invisible Hand: The Panic of 2007.* Oxford University Press.

Gorton, Gary B., and Ellis W. Tallman. 2018. *Fighting Financial Crises: Learning from the Past.* University of Chicago Press.

Gourinchas, Pierre-Olivier, Thomas Philippon, and Dimitri Vayanos. 2016. "The Analytics of the Greek Crisis." *NBER Macroeconomics Annual,* 31: 1–81.

Hartmann, Philip, and Frank Smets. 2018. "The First Twenty Years of the European Central Bank: Monetary Policy." *Brookings Papers on Economic Activity,* Fall.

Kaminsky, Graciela L., Carmen M. Reinhart, and Carlos A. Végh. 2003. "The Unholy Trinity of Financial Contagion." *Journal of Economic Perspectives,* 17(4): 51–74.

Kindleberger, Charles P. 1978. *Manias, Panics, and Crashes.* John Wiley and Sons.

Lane, Philip R. 2012. "The European Sovereign Debt Crisis." *Journal of Economic Perspectives,* 26(3): 49–68.

McKay, Alisdair, and Ricardo Reis. 2016. "The Role of Automatic Stabilizers in the U.S. Business Cycle." *Econometrica,* 84(1): 141–194.

Mishkin, Frederic S. 1999. "Lessons from the Tequila Crisis." *Journal of Banking and Finance,* 23(10): 1521–1533.

Montiel, Peter J. 2014. *Ten Crises.* Routledge.

Obstfeld, Maurice. 2013. "Finance at the Center Stage: Some Lessons of the Euro Crisis." *European Economy,* 493.

Ongena, Steven, Alexander Popov, and Neeltje Van Horen. 2019. "The Invisible Hand of the Government: Moral Suasion during the European Sovereign Debt Crisis." *American Economic Journal: Macroeconomics,* 11(4): 346–79.

Quinn, William, and John D. Turner. 2020. *Boom and Bust.* Cambridge University Press.

Rachel, Lukasz, and Lawrence Summers. 2019. "On Secular Stagnation in the Industrialized World." *Brookings Papers on Economic Activity,* 1: 1–73.

Radelet, Steven, and Jeffrey D. Sachs. 1998. "The East Asian Financial Crisis: Diagnosis, Remedies, Prospects." *Brookings Papers on Economic Activity,* (1): 1–90.

Ramey, Valerie A. 2019. "Ten Years after the Financial Crisis: What Have We Learned from the Renaissance in Fiscal Research?" *Journal of Economic Perspectives,* 33(2): 89–114.

Ramey, Valerie A., and Sarah Zubairy. 2018. "Government Spending Multipliers in Good Times and in Bad: Evidence from US Historical Data." *Journal of Political Economy,* 126(2): 850–901.

Ravn, Morten O., and Vincent Sterk. 2017. "Job Uncertainty and Deep Recessions." *Journal of Monetary Economics,* 90: 125–141.

Reinhart, Carmen M., and Kenneth S. Rogoff. 2009. *This Time is Different: Eight Centuries of Financial Folly.* Princeton University Press.

Reis, Ricardo. 2013. "The Portuguese Slump and Crash and the Euro Crisis." *Brookings Papers on Economic Activity,* 46(1): 143–210.

Reis, Ricardo. 2016. "Funding Quantitative Easing to Target Inflation." In *Designing Resilient Monetary Policy Frameworks for the Future.* Jackson Hole Symposium: Federal Reserve Bank of Kansas City.

Santos, Tano. 2017. "El Diluvio: The Spanish Banking Crisis, 2008–12." Columbia University manuscript.

Scheinkman, Jose A. 2014. *Speculation, Trading, and Bubbles.* Columbia University Press.

Shleifer, Andrei, and Robert Vishny. 2011. "Fire Sales in Finance and Macroeconomics." *Journal of Economic Perspectives,* 25(1): 29–48.

Sturzenegger, Federico, and Jeromin Zettelmeyer. 2006. *Debt Defaults and Lessons from a Decade of Crises.* MIT Press.

INDEX

Argentina, 5; 2001 crisis of, 68, 70
asset-backed securities, 36–37
asset prices, 1, 32, 47, 115; rapid fall of, 46

banking crises, 6, 65, 71
Bank of Japan, 7, 97–99
bank risk, 68
banks: modern, 34–35, 37, 43, 46, 101;
    modern and shadow, 33, 35; private, 36,
    60; traditional, 33, 35; undercapitalized,
    46
bonds, 96; of Argentina, 70
borrowers, 21, 34, 44, 53, 55–56
bubbles, 3, 17, 43, 115; asset prices and, 3, 14,
    25; attacks on, 16–17; beliefs and, 13, 15;
    boom phase of, 14, 18 credit-financed,
    20; extrapolative expectations and, 15;
    financial liberalization and, 4; hedge
    funds, 19; Hyman Minsky view of, 14;
    Internet 1998, 18, 20; Japan mid-1980s, 18;
    Keynes's view of, 13–14, 37; price path of,
    15; real estate, 17, 20; sophisticated traders
    and, 16; speculative asset, 13; speculators
    and, 13–14, 43
budget deficits, 105–6

Cajas, 5, 39
capital flows, 5, 28, 30; allocation of, 21, 25;
    debt contracts and, 53; flight to safety
    and, 73, 77; foreign investment and, 86;
    Spanish credit boom and, 37
capital inflows, 21, 25, 31, 89, 115
capital misallocation, 4, 21–22, 24–25, 27,
    30, 37

central banks, 7, 49, 65, 71; 2008 financial
    crisis and, 99; dual mandate of, 93;
    interest rates and, 96; as lenders of last
    resort, 94; reserve satiation and, 94, 97
Chile, 4, 28, 30, 52
Citigroup, 37
construction, 21–22, 26–27, 49
Covid-19 pandemic, 2, 8, 79, 106–7
creditors, 61, 63
currency: depreciation of, 50, 87–88,
    92; nominal interest rate and, 106;
    speculative attacks and, 51

Danatbank, 59–60
debt: default risk and, 65; emerging
    economies and, 84, 90; financial frictions
    and, 54–55; restructuring of, 75; solvency
    crises and, 58, 60
debt contracts, 5, 53, 55–56
default probability, 57, 68
deposit insurance, 32, 39, 59
diabolic loop, 67–68, 77
domestic goods, 83, 88

economic recoveries, 83–84, 88, 91, 115;
    Great Depression and, 109, 111
emerging economies, 6–7, 24, 28, 79, 84
entrepreneurs, 55, 105
euro, 4, 26–27, 76–77
euro crisis 2010, 6, 26, 37, 100
European banks, 6, 36–37, 39, 47–48, 51,
    67, 100
European Central Bank (ECB), 7, 61, 77, 93,
    100–101